Judge Sam'

'JUDGE SAM'

by SAMUEL H. SILBERT
with Sidney A. Eisenberg

CHANNEL PRESS

MANHASSET, NEW YORK

In memory of my mother,
  Miriam Silbert

~~~~~~

LIBRARY OF CONGRESS CATALOG CARD NUMBER: 63-19919

Printed in the United States of America

Table of Contents

CHAPTER 1

AT THE CORNER OF JUSTICE
– AND MARKET

MY FIRST memory of life in the United States goes back to 1889 or 1890. I was six years old—seven at the most. And tiny. Full grown, I've never reached five foot four. I spoke only a few words of English; I was an immigrant boy.

The memory involves justice and an urchin. I was selling newspapers on the corner of Market and Mulberry Streets in Newark, New Jersey. An older boy—perhaps he was twelve—elbowed me off my regular spot. His name was Big Boston, and in my mind he still assumes the shape of a lumbering giant. If Big Boston took over my corner, the day's papers would go unsold. And if they did, my mother and my sisters and I would again have to go without dinner. We were that poor.

Eyes blurred with tears of fury and frustration, I kicked and tore at Big Boston. But Justice, in the form of Officer Tom Moore, wasn't far down the street. He swaggered over, separated us, and with a kick and a curse sent Big Boston dodging away.

Justice. Questions of possession and envy and disregard for other's rights—matters of the way in which one seeks to attain his goal. Such are the questions that have dominated my days for many of the more than eighty years of a good, full and challenging life.

A great many newspapers have recently said—and in so saying have apparently gone unchallenged—that I have now served on the bench for more years than any other living American. Length of service, of course, is most of all a happy accident—a combination of sound health plus popularity with a usually fickle electorate. Quality of service, on the other hand, cannot be achieved accidentally. As I go to court each morning it is with the awareness that I will again have to struggle to find the fragile, elusive thing we call justice.

This book is most of all a report of my life with justice, my attempt to find it and understand it and administer it. I've gotten to know justice on relaxed, friendly, familiar terms—at the street level, in shirtsleeves, in the home. For a hundred thousand Americans I've been the sole point or perhaps the chief point of contact, during their lifetimes, with courtroom justice. With the law of our country.

That is a thought which astonishes me, which gives me pause, as I write it.

I began the practice of the law in 1907; the first case I ever argued concerned an attachment. My law partner and I, who had formed our partnership right after we received our degrees, walked into court and blithely presented our case. We didn't know much about our subject and we didn't think much of our opponent. Our client, we believed, had not been fairly treated in a business transaction. We expected to correct the wrong.

In Cleveland of the 1900's, law and the practice of law were far different from the protective, balanced, carefully charted system in use today. Matters now settled by qualified men working along well-defined lines were then handled in the Justice of the Peace (or "J.P.") courts. The Justice of the Peace received no salary. He depended on fees to maintain or better his standard of living. The office was elective and was considered a plum.

What "J.P." really stood for, we used to say, was "Judgment for the Plaintiff." Since the defendant had to pay court costs, the only way the Justice could be sure of collecting his fee was to render a verdict in favor of the plaintiff.

We were not aware of this, my partner and I, when we argued our case, presenting our reasonable notions. When we had concluded, our opponent simply rose to his feet and moved that our attachment be dissolved. The Justice granted the motion.

I looked at my partner, he looked at me, and then he asked, "Sam, what do we do now?"

"How the hell do I know?" I replied bitterly. "Let's ask a lawyer."

Losing that first case was painful in many ways. I needed the money; I needed a success that would attract other clients. But most of all, I needed *success*.

My life until 1907 had been formless and frequently futile.

I was born in Riga, Latvia, on April 15, 1883, the first of four children. Father, who was a teacher, was known in the community for his ability as an orator; he was described by my mother and family friends as a reformer, as a man who asked searching questions. Although our cottage floor was bare, he had a large library and is said to have read incessantly. To him, a good book open on one's lap was the pinnacle of achievement, and he called his books our treasury.

On one summer day we went swimming. Vividly I remember that my father floated on his back with me perched on his chest. I was happy "on the boat." Then the next day, I am told, he died. His appendix ruptured, and the doctor's assistant didn't know what to do.

When father died, we moved; then we sold our cow. Then our calf. Finally the struggle for existence was such that mother decided we would have to sell the books or go without the necessities of life. Even then, with four small children, the money she received would be no more than a stop-gap. She decided to use the receipts to take the family to America.

Soon after we reached New York we were told by the relatives who were harboring us that we might do better "in the country." And since in those days, everything west of the Hudson River was the "country," we moved to New Jersey.

The Newark we found in 1888 might just as well have been Latvia. Our basement apartment on Charles Street was cold and damp. Mother tried to make ends meet, mostly by sewing, but food was skimpy and the "money tree" of which we had heard in Riga quite obviously did not grow in our neighborhood. Those were the dark, lean days during which I tried to earn money for the family by selling *The Newark News, The Advertiser* and *The Sunday Call* on the corner of Mulberry Street.

The darkest day of all was a cold, drizzly Saturday when I was standing under an awning trying to get shelter as I counted up my profits. Until that moment it had been a pretty good day; to make a penny we had to sell two papers, and I had made twenty-nine cents that afternoon. Added to the twenty-five cents with which I had started, this made fifty-four cents in my pocket—more than enough to feed our family for a day.

As I was getting ready to start for home, a fine-looking man, smoking a long cigar, came along. He watched me put away the last pennies, then said, "Son, how would you like to earn a quarter?"

A quarter!

All I had to do, he explained, was deliver a note to a young lady on Trenton Street and return with her answer.

"The only thing is," the dapper man added, "how will I know that you won't just take my quarter and run off?"

I suggested that he needn't pay me until I returned. But for some reason which seemed plausible and acceptable to my youthful mind, this wasn't good enough for him. It was finally agreed that the gentleman would hold my fifty-four cents as security while I ran the errand.

Well, as you've probably guessed, both the gentleman and the fifty-four cents were gone when I returned from my useless search on Trenton Street.

I was badly hurt by that experience, and although I couldn't have put it in words, *caveat emptor*—let the buyer beware—became the first legal principle in my education.

One was either demolished in the competition on the corners of Newark or one became "street-wise"—able to sense impending disaster or sweet opportunity, able to hear a special language in the street sounds, able to spot the person planning to harm you or help you. If you were street-wise you could sort the truth from the rumor, the likely from the possible.

I learned to be street-wise, but I learned slowly. When this unusual sort of sensitivity became a part of my make-up, it was enormously helpful. Helpful to me when I served as a prosecuting attorney, helpful in my service on the bench. It was slow in coming not only because the language of the country was new, but because my thoughts were totally concentrated, day and night, on earning money for my family.

"Your family was the most impoverished family I have ever known," a friend named David Litter told me recently. Once a Newark newsboy himself, David Litter married Mary Sheck of Newark; her five brothers were also once fellow-newsies, peddling papers from other spots on Market Street. David, too, was a poor boy; now he heads a major chemical company, and serves as a member of the Mayor's Commission on Human Rights in New York. "Yes," he told me, "you were the poorest of all, Sam. Not enough to eat, not enough to wear, usually working for three hours before school and for eight hours after school."

All during the years I attended school—first at Morton Street, then Eighteenth Avenue, then back at Morton Street—I continued to peddle papers. The man who did the most for us newsboys was Jared Kimball, the superintendent of the Children's Aid Society, who was in charge of the Newsboys' Lodging House on Market Street. Kimball devoted his life to that home, making it a place where we could meet friends or play checkers, or simply enjoy warmth and companionship. When Kimball died, the home did, too, but before that I had the pleasure of meeting him again at a banquet in Newark given by friends in my honor when I was first elected judge.

I sold papers, watched over by Officer Moore, until the end of the Spanish American War, when the bottom dropped out of the paper market and I had to look for other work. Mike Hollander, whose father Adolph had a fur company—and whose brother Albert later invented the famous "Hollanderizing" process that was to make multi-millionaires of the family—was a friend and yet another fellow-newsboy. He got me a job as errand boy and general handyman with the family company.

When I finished the eighth grade I decided to quit school. My ambition then was to become a "flesher" with the Hollanders. A flesher made fantastic wages for those days—forty or fifty dollars a week. The flesher is the man who takes the animal skin as it comes from the trapper, with bits of flesh attached, and cleans it by running it over a stationary sharp knife. My mother decided this was no job for a youngster, so eventually I went back to selling newspapers at my old corner, but this time I had a stand, which was both more comfortable and more dignified.

During my boyhood years, I had one real, overriding ambition: to become, in spite of—or because of—my size, a professional boxer. My idol was a local boxer named Jimmy Handler, and when Jimmy told me that I "had the makings of a great fighter" there was no controlling me. Over my mother's strong demurrers, I began to train in earnest.

One of the ways I did this was to look for street fights. I found plenty of them. Thus in addition to making friends on the streets, I made a good many enemies, among them a group of the boys who decided to "get" me. They set up a match between me and a "hayseed" in a nearby basement. The newcomer was actually a professional from New York who outweighed me by ten pounds; I weighed all of ninety eight at the time. I didn't care much about the weight because I could always outrun him, but as soon as I realized what was afoot I should have had the brains to lie down. Instead, when I heard that the bets were against my lasting six rounds, I determined to last if it killed me. And although it didn't quite kill me, I did spend two weeks in the hospital, badly bruised and battered.

In the hospital my mother, who had always hated boxing, wept over what my life was becoming, a mixture of brutality and aimlessness. I was almost seventeen now, with not much of a present and no future. To help me make a new start, mother decided that our family should move to Denver, where we had a distant relative.

Denver sticks in my mind as the place where I first

learned the joys of playing the violin; certainly it did
not turn out to be the city where I was to make my
fortune. Our relative was a wholesale jeweler and he
gave me a job as a salesman and hired my brother,
Ben, as an errand boy. But business was bad and
within a year our boss had lost his money and I was
once again looking for new work.

I tried being a "train butcher," selling cigars, maga-
zines and candy between Denver and Grand Junction
on the Rio Grande. I hated everything about the work,
including the rough road-bed and the fact that I wasn't
making any money. It wasn't long before I quit.

About this time Ben, who had continued his school-
ing through high school and was interested in becoming an engineer, went to Mexico, where he got a job
with a friend. Mother decided to take my two sisters
and move to California. And I had heard of a job in
Cleveland with a jeweler. On the train, heading east,
I wondered how long it would be for this time.

In the old Union Depot, walking up the already
worn steps to the street, I found myself for the first
time in my life completely alone, a total stranger in
a strange city. I was frightened. I had no way of knowing I had come home at last.

Those early, penniless days in Cleveland were bitterly
hard ones. I went to claim my job at the jewelry store,
owned by two brothers named Arnstein. One was deaf
and the other dyspeptic, and the first day I almost lost
my job because of his temper. But it took only a thrust
of my hands into empty pockets to make me decide to
take whatever he wanted to offer and to come up
smiling. After all, the salary was seven dollars a week.

I didn't have the nerve to ask for a wage advance and I had no room, so I checked my belongings in the old Union Depot, God rest its buried and dingy soul, and slept upon the benches.

Several nights at the station gave me a sore back and enough courage to ask a fellow worker to loan me a dollar so that I could rent a room in a private home. Now I was firmly established: I had an address and a place to change my clothes, and a job at Arnstein Bros. & Mier.

In the early 1900's, food wasn't too much of a problem if you had a little nerve. All you had to do was go into a saloon, order a beer, then eat all the free lunch you could until the menacing eyes of the bartender said it would be wise to move on. (If I was still hungry I'd repeat the maneuver at the next saloon, and eat to my heart's content.)

As I settled into my job and a routine, I began to realize that I needed more than food to be happy. I had gone through only the first eight grades at school, spending most of the rest of my time on street corners. I had never read a good book. My grammar was poor and my vocabulary limited. But I remembered a parting promise to my mother to try to educate myself. I attended lectures, joined debating societies and read, read and read. Finally, discontented with my slow progress, I saved up a few dollars and enrolled in Central Institute, a Cleveland night school.

So now I would put in long days at the store, perhaps twelve hours with a half-hour off for lunch, and then rush home to change clothes before going to school. After two years of this I went to Judge Willis Vickery, dean of the Cleveland Law School, a night law college. I explained that I wanted to become a lawyer and that I would like to attend law school on those nights when I did not have to attend classes at the Central Institute.

The judge, a fierce-looking man with bristling gray hair and stern gray eyes, studied me hard as he tried to dissuade me from this man-killing schedule. After all, to add a law course would give me but five or six hours a day in which to study law *and* sleep. But I begged and the judge agreed to let me try.

It still wasn't enough. While I could handle the subjects at law school, my use of words and my pronunciation sometimes made me the butt of ridicule. So I put in extra time on grammar books and practically slept with a dictionary. Suddenly a saturation point was reached; even I had to admit that the schedule was too full. I persuaded my employers to retain me on a half-day basis at the jewelry store. They agreed, and reduced my salary by only one dollar a week, so that I still earned a dollar a day.

With no money worries and with so much more time for study, I was the valedictorian of my class when graduation day at Central Institute arrived. Nights at law school were also much easier. My grammar had improved and my marks were high enough so that I was graduated *cum laude*. We were given our diplomas by Newton D. Baker, who was to become mayor of Cleveland and then Secretary of War in World War I. He singled me out for special mention, speaking of my struggle and progress in this land of ours.

The year was 1907. I took the bar examination and passed it, and there I was—an attorney at law.

CHAPTER 2

THE LAWYERS AND
THE SQUIRES

NOW, I FEEL, we can begin to talk about the law. The swearing in, so to speak, has been concluded. You know my name and address and profession.

Let's just muse, first, about the practice of law before the men we called Squires, the Justices of the Peace.

One of my first clients was a lady of little virtue by the name of Fanny. Fanny got into trouble, a not unusual occurrence for women of her trade, and was summoned to J.P. court. One day, I went to see the Justice who was assigned to hear her case. Forgetting to knock, I walked in to find my client sitting in the lap of justice. Fanny, of course, was not embarrassed. And the Squire had presence of mind: "Well," he said, "a fellow has to collect court costs, doesn't he?"

Mr. Callaghan, a mover, had performed his services

for a woman who was one of the city's notorious dead-beats. He had not, of course, been paid. After trying half a dozen lawyers, he somehow finally came to me. And as an incentive he offered to give me all his collection business if I could collect this one bill.

Since this would be the first real taste of money, I went to work with vigor, but didn't get at all farther than had any of my predecessors. However, I wanted Callaghan's business so much that I sent him a check of my own for what the woman owed him, less my fee, representing it as a successful collection. Callaghan was jubilant. My conscience was unhappy, though, and I confessed.

I've always liked Callaghan. He just laughed at my ingenuity, and then gave me his business anyway.

On another occasion I had a large note to collect from two wealthy brothers who were what we called "execution proof"—which meant, for all practical purposes, that although they had the money, no one could find it in order to attach it.

In the normal course of events, I took a judgment against the brothers, but they paid no more attention to me than to anyone else who tried to part them from their money. However, fortified with my court order, I decided to do something about it, specifically to put in a "keeper," a person who stays on the premises to seek assets.

The keeper I selected was a courthouse character we called—for good reason—"Onion Pete." Pete ate onions and drank whiskey for breakfast; he drank whiskey and ate onions for lunch; he snacked on onions in the afternoon, and washed them down with

whiskey when other people were having dinner. When
Onion Pete walked into a room, he didn't need a
calling card to announce his presence. This was the
keeper I had picked for the brothers.

They were horrified. Onion Pete would smell up
their elegant offices and would ruin their business
(they had a high-class clientele). The brothers demanded that I find a keeper more in keeping with the
premises; instead I mentioned that Pete liked to munch
on onions as others might on apples.

The brothers settled. And, like Mr. Callaghan, they
too became clients of mine for as long as I was a
practicing lawyer.

My client was being sued. He had ordered a coffin
for a relative, but he didn't pay for it. Obviously, I
knew we had no defense—but I also knew that in J.P.
court no defense was often the best defense.

The plaintiff presented his case; he had built the
coffin my client had ordered and had not been paid.

It was our turn next. Trying my best to keep a
straight face, I claimed defective workmanship. Why
that coffin was so poorly constructed, Your Honor, that
cold air would come right through the cracks!

Prove it? In J.P. court who asked for proof? The
Squire laughed out loud and laughed the case right
out of court.

Legal fees in the early 1900's were not very lucrative,
and if we didn't collect in advance we rarely collected
at all. Five or ten dollars was the most we could expect
and often we made four or five appearances in court
before we earned such fees. Of course, our expenses

weren't very great either. The cost of an office was nominal. The average pay of a stenographer was about two dollars a week, and a full course meal could be had for about twenty-five cents, including strudel for dessert.

I was defending a chap by the name of Goldman who had had his wages attached by a man named Berkman. Berkman claimed that Goldman had jumped a twenty-eight dollar board bill. The eagle was spreading his wings toward an oratorical heaven, when the constable entered, and interrupted.

"Goldman quit working the day that we garnisheed him," said the constable. "All we got is a dollar seventy-five."

"I get that for defending him," I said quickly.

"No, you don't," said Berkman. "He owes that to me."

"You're both wrong," said the Squire. "That money goes to the court for the Justice's fees."

And he put the money into his pocket.

My law practice varied with the needs of my clients. I drew up contracts and agreements, defended criminals and handled divorce cases. On one occasion I had a vagrancy case before one of our judges, who astonishingly set a $200,000 bail on my client. I protested vehemently. "Don't be so disturbed," the Judge remonstrated. "I did it to compliment him. He couldn't even raise twenty dollars, so I made the bail $200,000 just to make him feel good."

And then there was a case involving forty-five dollars and a horse, and don't ask me what it was all about.

Neither of the parties could speak English very well, but the case was hotly contested. The weather was hot, too, and the Justice was having a difficult time controlling his temper.

When the evidence was finally presented and it came time for the closing arguments, the lawyers each insisted upon three hours for their summations. Faced with six more hours of oratory, the Squire rose, turned to the lawyers and said, "If you each want three hours for argument, take three hours for argument. If you want my decision, it is in my drawer. If you want me, I am in the saloon downstairs."

My client was seeking a divorce. The grounds were desertion, which had to have been for a period of over three years in order to be valid. But when my client took off her coat in the courtroom, both the Judge and I could see that she was unquestionably pregnant. The Judge looked at the woman, then looked at me. I tried the case as though I were a blind man. Since the matter was uncontested the Judge decided to overlook the slightly enlarged anatomy of my client and granted her a divorce.

In one incredible case, a defendant was about to be bound over to the Grand Jury for murder. However, he had a very ingenious lawyer, who depended a great deal upon the colossal ignorance of the Squires. The lawyer stood up in court and moved that the prisoner be discharged. The defendant thought that this was such a good idea that he got up and seconded the motion of his counsel.

The Justice was stumped, and called a recess to find

out what to do. It was suggested by the defense lawyer that the Squire put the question to a vote. The Justice thereupon resumed court and inquired, "All in favor of the defendant being discharged will say, 'Aye.'"

The lawyers and the prisoner at the bar both promptly said "Aye."

Then the Squire asked for those opposed, and the constable said "Nay."

With that, the Squire solemnly said: "The majority being in favor of dismissal, the defendant is herewith discharged."

I was cleaning out my office, winding up my private practice, when a gang of toughs marched in. They'd known me in the early years when I had defended them, successfully, in an assault and battery case. They had had no money for a fee.

Now they wanted to repay me, they said. With that one of them opened the door to call in a famed lady-of-the-streets generally known as "Dirty Denah."

"We still don't have any money so we brought Denah," the spokesman said. "She's yours for the day."

I mounted a chair, made a graceful speech of thanks and concluded with a flourish: "Boys, I make you a present of my fee."

CHAPTER 3

POLICE PROSECUTOR, ABOVE THE STABLE

FOUR YEARS after I was graduated from law school I gave up the private practice of law, never, as events developed, to return to it. The year was 1911 and Newton D. Baker, then city solicitor and mayor-elect —the man who had spoken so kindly of me at my graduation—appointed me to the police prosecutor's office. What a place it was in those days!

In an outer lobby the complainants sat, argued and even fought as they waited in turn to see us. Our offices, three small rooms, were indescribably filthy, and the only courtroom in the building was a noise-filled hall located, with some appropriateness, at the end of a corridor above a stable. The judge sat behind a brass rail on an elevation in the packed, foul courtroom. Prisoners were brought before him and their cases disposed of in a confusion of rapid mutterings and garbled language, inaudible to the spectators. The judge was free to do just about what he wished.

I took the desk formerly occupied by George P. Baer, who had been elevated to the judiciary and who has since passed on. I asked Judge Baer if he had any advice.

"You will find that the boys in here like to loaf," he said, "but my advice is that you work hard and keep working, working, working. Remember that you were placed here to listen to the complaints of your fellow men. Their problems, no matter how trivial they seem to you, are important to them—and the last ragamuffin waiting in that line is just as important as the first."

My very first case as police prosecutor had an odd coincidental ring. A policeman came to ask me to issue a warrant for arrest.

"I picked up this kid for vagrancy," he said. "He hasn't committed any crime but he's been sleeping on the benches at Union Station. He has no money, no job, no means of support. In fact," the officer concluded confidently, "he don't have nobody. Ya got nothing to worry about."

Instead of issuing the warrant I told the puzzled officer to bring the boy from his cell to my office. The youngster's story was an echo from my past. On his way to Buffalo, he had run out of funds, and so he was using the Cleveland railroad station for a hotel.

"Young man!" I gave him as stern a look as I could, "Are you trying to take my job from me?"

Then I explained to the startled youth and to the policeman how, not so many years before, I too had used the depot benches for my bed. Next I called a friend, who promised to get the boy a job. This was my first taste of the happiness and pride I still feel whenever I am in a position to prevent an injustice.

As it turned out, I was able not only to keep a boy (who shouldn't have been arrested in the first place) from going to jail, but to give the community a man who has been an outstanding citizen these many years.

Even then, on my first day in the job, I didn't believe it was the sole aim of a prosecutor to prosecute, much less to persecute. I believed prosecutors should be counselors and friends. I sought to heal rather than to hurt, and I am still trying.

One morning, as I was about to go into court to prosecute what seemed to me a minor case, a lawyer dropped in to discuss it with me. I couldn't understand his anxiety about the defendant and I cut our talk short. As the man stood up to go we shook hands. When I released mine, it held a $1,000 bill.

We didn't earn much as prosecutors; that bill almost equaled my annual salary. I stood there for a moment, numb, faced for the first time with bribery. Then my fury found its tongue and I lashed out at the man, telling him what I'd do to him after I finished with his client in court.

Bursting with anger, I stormed into court and tore into the defendant as though his case were a matter of life and death. The judge couldn't understand why I was so disturbed about a routine situation. In fact, he thought so little of the whole thing that he let the defendant go free. The briber must have been pleased with himself; he still had his $1,000 which could not be mentioned by me in the course of this particular case. And his client had his freedom. I had only my righteous indignation—until some months later, when

—alerted by this incident—we trapped the attorney in his next attempt at bribery.

Not long after that episode I was visited in the evening by a man involved in a case I was taking into court the next day. He had a very simple request:

"I just want you to make sure that justice prevails," he said.

"What do you call justice?" I inquired.

"Justice? Deciding for me, not the other fellow. Mix the whole thing up and then throw him out."

"You'll get justice, all right," I promised. He beamed, not catching the tone of my voice. As he left he shook hands and left a twenty-dollar gold piece in my palm. I lost my temper and ordered him from my house.

He was puzzled but apologetic. Humbly he said, "Mr. Prosecutor, it ain't right to give you twenty dollars?"

"Of course not."

He glanced around in a hush-hush manner and then whispered, "If twenty dollars ain't right, how much *is* right?"

I was older and a lot more experienced before I learned that money was not the only coin of bribery. Many of the ways used to bribe judges and other public officials are far more subtle, and therefore more subversive. Not only can they not be proved in court, but often the honest judge who wouldn't dream of taking a bribe is unaware that he is being influenced. This kind of bribery takes the form of conferred social status—invitations, often to the wife, from people of a higher social or economic group; fellowship, and even friendship, bestowed by those who have either

an immediate or a long range need to influence a
judge.

The police prosecutor's office, with its colorful cases—
backyard squabbles, family fights, wife beaters, wife
neglecters, wife coveters, pimps and harlots—was a
favorite hangout for the city's reporters, most of whom
were a pretty tough, hard-drinking bunch in the typical "Front Page" style of the day. (As a matter of fact,
one of them, Al Bergener, then city editor of *The
Cleveland News*, was later immortalized as "Burns"
in that play.)

While waiting around for news, the reporters
amused themselves by conducting cockroach races,
and they once invited me to be a judge. I was honored
until I discovered that a cockroach race, with its slow,
zig-zagging "runners" and its complicated rulings on
what is or isn't out of bounds, is an absolutely intermin-
able affair. I resigned before the first race was ever
concluded.

The reporters were eventually joined by a frail,
sandy-haired teenager, a timid little cub called Louie.
The other men had the usual fun with him, sending
him off on fake assignments. Louie never complained,
though often, I thought, they overstepped the bounds
between a joke and harassment.

One day while I was questioning a dope pusher, the
criminal suddenly decided to name his co-conspirators
in a confession. I needed a witness, and quickly, in the
event the confession was later recounted in court.

Not another person was around, just little Louie.
I had no confidence at all that he could do the job, but
I took him down to the bull pen with me and handed

him a pad and paper. "Write down everything he says," I ordered.

I got all through with my questioning before I saw that Louie hadn't taken a note. That seemed to be that. A great, once-in-a-lifetime opportunity lost. I stormed off.

Then in the next day's paper, there was the dope pusher's story, almost word for word the way he told it. And that is how I gave Louis Seltzer, editor of *The Cleveland Press*, his first big story. How I "gave" him another—much bigger—story is quite another thing, but by then I was a judge and he was an editor, and that is a subject for a later chapter.

Those years in the prosecutor's office were hectic, hardworking ones, and the line of complainants that paraded past our desks never seemed to end. In the four years that I held the job, I heard almost 75,000 complaints. I issued 6,800 summonses and, I estimated, settled more than 40,000 cases amicably in the office. My colleagues dubbed me "The Great Compromiser."

Of the thousands of cases, a few stick in my mind, mostly because of the people who were involved. One of these was an actress, fighting mad, infuriated by the fact that every day her father-in-law teased her for being cross-eyed.

I gave her a mirror and told her to look into it.

"Do you think it's true?"

"Of course not!" she flamed.

"Then why bother about his twisted humor? If you have straight eyes, he can't cross them."

A man was brought in for calling a certain girl names

every time he walked by her house. He was ordered to stop and he promised that he would, but he found a technical loophole. He didn't *call* her names from then on; instead he *sang* his insults whenever he went past her house.

Back they came to court again. Perhaps he was the forerunner of the singing commercials.

A woman came to the office screaming, "My neighbor called me a whore and I demand that she prove it!"

I called in the neighbor and argued her into giving the woman a written apology. In ludicrous solemnity I watched her write, "She is not a whore." I handed the document to the "not whore," who walked out triumphantly with her husband.

A complainant wanted a man arrested for assault and battery. "For no reason at all," he said, "this man hits me some hard punches, Mr. Prosecutor. And then when he gets all done, he hands me this card with his name on it. I want him arrested."

I looked at the card and at the signature, John Doe, scrawled across it. Our complainant was indignant when we told him that we couldn't arrest John Doe because there was no such person. "There *must* be," he insisted. "Just take a look at this eye."

The people who came to our office were mainly of foreign extraction. They sat in the lobby for hours and waited patiently to tell us their stories in pursuit of what they considered their rights.

In broken, halted English they recited their difficulties. Often these were backyard squabbles, tales of brutal husbands or parents, instances where the quarrels of children resulted in the parents' remaining enemies long after the youngsters were friends again.

Dogs caused terrible complications; they were always being fought over. I recall two men who came in and argued bitterly about the ownership of a dog. I had the coveted animal, a friendly mutt, brought into my office.

"Here, Victor," one man called, and the dog ran to him.

"Here, Tommy," the other beckoned, and the dog eagerly responded.

"Here, Honus," I cried. You guessed it. The pup ran to me.

I don't remember who finally got the dog. But the pooch caused me a miserable day.

Some of the immigrants got into difficulties because of the ignorance of the laws. One couple terminated their marriage by the very simple expedient of tearing up their license. They felt that this ended the matter. (After having heard some 80,000 divorce cases, I sometimes wonder if they weren't right.)

Another husband didn't even bother to tear up the marriage license. He simply walked out, remarried and left his first wife and three children to shift for themselves. By the time I made the wife's acquaintance, the man had a family by his second wife, too. I could see no advantage in having him jailed, thereby leaving two families without support, so I recommended that the first wife get a divorce. Her support from the light-footed former mate was meager and she came to see me regularly, saying, "At least you listen to my troubles." One day while she was telling me those troubles, I received this letter from a man whose complaints I had unwrinkled previously:

Dear Mr. Silbert: I want to get married. I know you are a man who has good taste, so please pick me out a nice lady. I don't want a lady who is too young because I am forty myself. But I don't want and old one. I will leave it to your judgment.

I looked up at the woman and asked, "Would you like to get married?"

"Get married?" she repeated, startled. "I don't know." Then she asked, "To what kind of a man?"

"He's a very nice man and he'll make you a good husband. Wait a few minutes and I'll have him speak for himself."

My clerk went and fetched the man, who worked nearby. I introduced them and went into the adjoining office. Before the hour was over we were joined by a justice of the peace.

It was fun serving as best man. But right after it was over the woman paled and took me aside.

"My God!" she exclaimed. "I'm afraid it's all spoiled. We were so excited I forgot to tell him I have three children." I took the man aside and tried to break the news to him gently. To my surprise, his face shone with joy.

"That's all right," he said. "That makes us even. I've got three children of my own that I forgot to say anything about."

I like to think they had a wonderful life together—and as far as I know, they did.

As a police prosecutor, I really felt I had "arrived," so I wasn't particularly surprised when, one day, a well set-up man came to my office and said, "Mr. Prosecutor, you're getting known nationally, what with all the good work you are doing in this office."

I was flattered.

"We're issuing a book about the famous people in all the big cities, and we want you in it. You can write your biography yourself if you want to. We feel you have had a remarkable career."

Obviously I should have wondered what was so remarkable about the career of a young police prosecutor—except to himself—but this was still the gullible Sam who left his fifty-four cents with the stranger as "security" while he ran an errand up Trenton Street.

"Our regular price is $100," the salesman continued. "But we'll give you a special price of eighty dollars."

For weeks and even months afterwards I don't think there was a day I didn't eagerly await the mail, looking for my book of famous Americans. And one day it finally arrived. Sure enough, there was the beautiful biography, just as I had written it, all nicely done and topped with a picture of myself. And right next to mine was an equally handsome biography and picture of Arbut, the bootlegger.

It was a long, long time before that stopped being a great joke around the police prosecutor's office.

In the prosecutor's office warrants were issued as a matter of course, with no thought that there might be another road to settlement than arrest. It was much better, I thought, to try preliminary arbitration. I argued long for it and finally my superiors acquiesced;

they set up a conciliation court and a conciliation branch of the prosecutor's office as a temporary measure. Fifty years later it is still doing a flourishing business.

Another injustice that disturbed me was the manner in which arrests were made. On the lightest complaint, justified or not, the old Black Maria would roll up in front of the house of a respectable citizen and bring him to us. I started a system of having these people come before us in response to a written summons, placing personal bond to assure their later appearance. In this way many folks had their day in court without so much attendant humiliation and shame. This system, too, is still in effect.

During my tenure in the prosecutor's office the state enacted an eight-hour-a-day labor law, one honored almost solely in the breach. In order to try to put teeth into the legislation, I swore out a warrant against one notorious violator. After he was convicted the law was no longer regarded as a joke.

But my two most satisfying projects as prosecutor were the stamping out of phony employment agencies and the smashing (temporarily, of course) of dope traffic in Cleveland.

Our large foreign-born population, unaccustomed to our ways and unfamiliar with our language, were particularly at the mercy of unscrupulous employment agencies. Their operation was diabolically simple: they just offered jobs which did not exist, collecting their fees from the gullible applicants in advance.

The fees were in cash and the agencies gave no receipts. How could you prove anything against them? Applicants who demanded refunds were abused and even subjected to violence. Other unscrupulous agencies made agreements with certain employers, who would hire workers but then fire them as soon as the agencies had collected their fees.

These tricky, slimy people were licensed under the law. Rooting them out was tiring, thankless work, but I plugged away, rounding up witnesses, bringing in employers, confiscating records, until the operators of these shyster agencies were either in jail or had moved to some balmier climate. The newspapers were of invaluable help throughout this battle, giving the problem the airing it needed. After a year or so, the state legislature put more teeth in the law and our job was done.

Hundreds of dope cases passed through our office. Cocaine and heroin were peddled openly in saloons, pool rooms and even in drug stores. Still, the evidence was hard to obtain, for the laws on our books were almost totally ineffective.

In my last year in the prosecutor's office I was concerned almost exclusively with cleaning up Cleveland's traffic in drugs. This was 1915, the year Congress finally passed the Harrison Act, a law that provided for federal registration of drugs and for the prosecution of drug peddlers.

Headlines in 1915 declared that the United States was becoming a nation of "dope fiends," with more than 5,000,000 men and women afflicted by drugs. Estimates put the number of addicts in our city as high as 10,000, and while that may have been an exaggeration the point is that the situation was serious.

Our Pure Food and Drug laws were less stringent

then, and some unscrupulous manufacturers of soft drinks and patent medicines spiked their products with dope to secure repeat business, thus starting many a new victim on the downward spiral. Narcotics were sold to fat people with the promise that the drug would make them thin; to thin people on just the opposite pretext. The impotent were promised virility; the childless, fertility. No matter how he attracted his victim, the peddler's aim was to get him "hooked," and after that he just had to keep his customer supplied.

The first step in our crusade was to halt the open sales of narcotics and to collar the peddlers. This was the easiest part. Ferreting out the higher-ups was, as always, more difficult. But as our drive began to show results, the hardships began to affect the poor devils who suddenly found themselves without their needed drugs. They streamed into our offices, abusive or weeping and begging for help. We set up a cure for them at our city institution at Warrensville, and many actually were helped.

As we got deeper and deeper into this investigation, cooperating with both the police and the federal agents, we learned that the ring operating in our city was not purely local, but extended as far east as Pennsylvania and west to Toledo and Chicago. I was put in charge of our investigation and by the time we had completed our drive we had arrested and convicted 249 peddlers.

When we began sending the peddlers to jail, I began to get threats to my life, usually by telephone. A newspaper headline, "Prosecutor Silbert's Life Threatened by Dope Fiend," brought me an offer of help

from a very tough citizen, one whom I had once befriended. "Just give me the name of any man in this
town you want killed," he said, "and I'm the boy who
will do the job."

As the year ended and the estimated number of
drug addicts had dropped to about 1,000, we learned
what is well known today—that narcotics and crime
are interwoven. With our drug racket curtailed, our
crime rate was cut almost in half.

Cases in the police prosecutor's office were seldom
carefully prepared. Thus we had a stream of acquittals
because of technical loopholes or failure to marshall
the proper evidence. I suggested to our Safety Direc-
tor that we could correct some of our inadequacies,
and he gave me a free hand to set up what I believe
was the first series of lecture courses for any police
department in the country. Outstanding experts were
assigned to instruct policemen on how to gather evidence when making an arrest, so that the court follow-
through could be effective.

It was not just seeing our record of convictions
mount that made me proud; it was reading that many
other cities adopted the same methods of strengthen-
ing the administration of justice.

We still have lawyers and prosecutors who fail to
prepare their cases properly, and defendants who are
released because of technicalities. Fortunately the
number is less each year and our communities become
safer, happier places in which to live.

CHAPTER 4

POLITICS MAKES A PATH
TO THE BENCH

MY FIRST foray into politics was in 1909, when I decided to run for city councilman. It was one of my two unsuccessful quests for public office, and although neither was politically fatal, I learned a lot from each defeat. In 1909 I had neither the experience nor the following needed to win. In fact, by the time I decided to enter the primary, the Democrats already had a candidate. I couldn't help but lose, only I wasn't smart enough to know it at the time.

The key district in the fifteenth ward, in which I had decided to run, had the distinction of being one of the worst in the city. There were saloons on every corner and, more often than not, several in between.

"It'll get you votes if you help the boys rush the growler," somebody told me.

Translated, this simply meant that I was supposed to supply free beer to the boys in the neighborhood. My "supporters" would call their meetings in the basement of somebody's home, order beer by the bucket and pass it from mouth to mouth. I was to pay the bill and, hopefully, collect the votes.

Well, if that was the way to do it, I would so do it! Most of the basements in that precinct were vile and the men were pretty rugged. I surrounded myself with a couple of the toughest boys in the neighborhood so that I would have might, as well as right, with me. This seemed to help keep peace in the cellars. My most effective bodyguard was Archie Stone, one of the champion fighters in the ward.

Women did not yet have the right to vote so one had to go where the men were, to saloons. I remember walking into one saloon and plunking down a twenty-dollar bill with a flourish. I told the bartender to give everyone a shot on their next councilman.

He poured out the whiskey. And an extra for himself. Then he picked up the twenty, said "That's just right," and put it in the cash drawer.

From then on I carried money in smaller denominations. I learned, too, that a thirsty voter did not mean a committed voter.

The political boss of the ward was the late John Sulzman, who eventually became county sheriff. He was a shrewdly gentle, gray-haired man who had a kind word for everybody.

"How is your darlin' old mother?" he would ask, whether he knew you or your darlin' old mother or not. This got votes, I found out. And I remembered it.

John owned a cigar store in the district then. As the campaign drew to a close he summoned me to his store. He told me he admired the spirited fight I was putting up but that I wouldn't make it. People knew and liked the regular candidate. The Party was backing him.

I didn't believe it; look at all the "voters" I was meeting in the basements and saloons.

Tom L. Johnson, who is still considered one of the greatest mayors Cleveland ever had, also called me in for a talk, and also asked me to withdraw in favor of the party candidate. I refused, bluntly and to the point of arrogance. I have always been sorry that I made such a poor impression on the great Mayor that day.

In the meantime I was stepping up my own campaign. I printed handbills and paid some of my workers fifteen cents a day to hand them out. Three of the boys so paid grew up to be the millionaire Lampl Brothers—Joe, Jack and Carl. Then on primary day I collected my little band of followers, and we went from corner to corner, campaigning to the last. For each speech the applause was terrific. Of course, the audiences' appreciation of my speeches was somewhat lubricated by the barrels of beer I had thoughtfully furnished.

In spite of common sense, I was sure I was a winner. Alas, the next day I discovered that my opponent had topped me by thirty-three votes. While I was buying beer and making speeches on Primary day, my opponent was doing the same thing. He, however, furnished his beer after the voters had whetted their thirst on mine—so it was his beer they remembered in the voting booths.

Well, if you can't beat 'em, do you join 'em? I thought not. Then wise John Sulzman helped me, showing me the importance at this time, when reform was needed,

of working with the Johnson forces. I joined our ward
club, campaigned for Tom L., and tried to make myself useful in general. (Johnson was defeated that year
by Herman Baeher, who served as mayor for one two-
year term.) In spite of my personal defeat and then
that of my party, I thoroughly enjoyed my novitiate in
politics, and I knew I would come back for more.

One other important event in my life took place in
1909—one far more successful than the attempt at
politics. That was the year that Miss Ann Weinstein—
whom I had met when I visited Steubenville on occa-
sional travels—and I were married. As a "Divorce
Judge," as I am sometimes called, I should probably
have important observations to make on our marriage,
but when you have been married and in love with the
same woman for fifty-four years, I think that speaks
for itself. Oddly enough, Ann and I have always been
temperamentally very different. I am extremely gregarious, I love people, all kinds of people, and I enjoy going to meetings and making speeches. I feel
perfectly at home wherever I go. Ann, on the other
hand, is shy and reserved and more dignified. She
always preferred to stay at home rather than to accompany me to the meetings and dinners and civic
affairs that I enjoy, and I know that she cannot understand why a man of eighty carries a fulltime work load.
But although we may be different, we have always
been together, and that is the only thing that counts.

Two years later, in 1911, I had no trouble supporting
the Democrat's candidate for Mayor. He was Newton
D. Baker, and he was the kind of man who, unfortunately, doesn't happen very often in public life.

Baker was an idealist, a thoroughly honest intellectual who loved public service. There was no pretense in his makeup; he was no seeker of favors. He despised politics in the mean sense of the word; he hated fakes and phonies. With all this, he was extremely human and not at all "untouchable." I believed in everything Mayor Baker stood for and I worked like a Trojan on his campaign. The week after his election he called me to his office, told me that he had been following my career, and he appointed me to the police prosecutor's staff. I was awed and flattered and I wrote a long letter to Ma that night, sharing my joy with her.

Baker was one of the new breed of speechifiers. To audiences brought up on William Jennings Bryan, he didn't sound like an orator at all. After one meeting that I attended with him in Chagrin Falls, a woman came up to shake his hand and said: "Mr. Baker, I liked your speech, but you ain't no orator."

"Why not?" Mr. Baker asked.

"Because you spoke so plain I understood every word you said," the woman explained.

Baker often said this was the greatest compliment on his speaking he ever received.

One of my favorite stories about Mayor Baker concerned a newsboy named Tommy who was always in trouble, mostly for gambling in the streets. On one of his many appearances in Juvenile Court, the tide seemed to be turning against him—until the street-wise lad got an idea.

"I want my lawyer," he said. The judge, somewhat taken aback, asked who his lawyer was.

"The mayor," Tommy announced. "Newton D. Baker."

Before becoming mayor, Baker had been a leading member of the Cleveland YMCA Social Service Club which launched so many welfare services in Cleveland—including the establishment of the very Juvenile Court in which Tommy was standing. In any event, the judge telephoned Baker, who not only appeared for Tommy but pledged himself responsible for the urchin's good behavior.

"If he gets in trouble again you both go to jail," the judge grinned.

It wasn't much later in the year that Tommy burst into Mayor Baker's office all out of breath and shouting: "Beat it, Mayor, the cops are after us again."

In 1915, after four years on the police prosecutor's staff, I decided to run for Municipal Court judge. I felt that my background qualified me as a candidate, and I was full of enthusiasm for the prospective campaign.

Our judges were nominated by petition and we would-be candidates needed 2,500 petition signatures to get our names on the ballot. Here, the thousands of persons I had met as a prosecutor were helpful. So were policemen and other city workers who had befriended me or had been befriended by me. Also I was reasonably well known among clubs and societies, and business and professional groups before which I had spoken.

When the names were counted I found that my petitions led all the others, with more than 25,000 qualified names.

Business was booming in our courts and the state legislature had created three new judicial posts. I had chosen to run for one of these newly-created terms so that I wouldn't have to compete against a judge already on the bench. This was a smart political move, which meant that I was not the only one who thought of it; others just as ambitious and as well-acquainted were in the race. Altogether there were twenty-eight of us running for the three new judicial offices. The three candidates who polled the largest number of votes would be elected. The unsuccessful twenty-five would have each other for comfort and solace.

This was no comfort to me—I didn't want solace. I wanted to be a judge.

In campaigning for my first judicial term I bore in mind the scars and mistakes of my unsuccessful venture for the City Council. There was much to do making new acquaintances and renewing old ones. But this time ward leaders treated me well and I found I had many friends in the Republican party as well as among Democrats.

Hoping for votes I attended a picnic of a large Irish society. My invitation came from a friend who was acting as chairman of the event and I was the only non-Irishman there. I don't know whether it was with the serious idea of getting me lots of votes or just for the fun of it, but the chairman insisted upon introducing me as "Prosecutor McSilbert."

After the meeting a man came up, shook my hand heartily and said:

"McSilbert, you sound like a regular sort of guy. You've got a fine Irish name, McSilbert, and I'll vote for you, but I'll be damned if you don't look like a Jew to me!"

At another meeting—I believe it was a labor union—I was sitting on the platform when a member got up and addressed the chair:

"Mr. Chairman, I move that we make Prosecutor Silbert a suspicious member of this organization."

In a twinkling I was suspiciously theirs.

I remember one evening, chasing from meeting to meeting to corral that last vote. When I got to "Starlight" Boyd's district I was dismayed to find the meeting was over. Starlight was one of the most influential "czars" reigning in Cleveland's Negro district, and I knew that in order to get the vote in this sector I would first have to gain his approval.

But the meeting was over, the room was empty. I went to the saloon downstairs where I spotted Boyd's imposing figure propped against the bar. I worked my way through the crowd to him, introduced myself and apologized for being late to his meeting. I stated my plea for his support.

He was silent. I squirmed.

"Will you have a drink, Mr. Starlight?" I finally asked.

"Sure I will," he said. Turning to the crowd, he boomed: "Boys, we've got Judge Silbert with us. Have a drink on the next judge."

They cheered and ordered up a gin with a beer wash as I gulped hard at the thought of my pocket's meager contents. Starlight hoisted me onto a beer barrel and asked me to say a few words.

I spoke for a couple of minutes, hardly making myself heard above the din and confusion. It was hot.

"How about another drink?" someone in the crowd yelled.

"Boys, have another drink on Judge Silbert," Starlight urged.

Though my own throat was parched and dry I refused a drink. I stood there in agony as everybody downed gin and beer, wondering how I could ever foot the bill. Starlight must have seen my anguished expression as I went fumbling through my pockets.

"You can't pay for any drinks here, now or any other time," he roared. "You are the one prosecutor who took care of me and my boys without regard to race or color. You treated us all honestly and fairly. We'll do all we can to help you."

And while I stumbled over the words of appreciation he shouted again: "Boys, have another drink on Judge Silbert." And they did. This time I put my foot on the brass rail and drank as heartily as the rest.

That expression, "Judge Silbert," rang in my ears all night long.

On Election Day I made the rounds of the city to check on how things were going. It was a pins-and-needles day for me.

That night at my headquarters, Tony, one of my most faithful workers, said he would check on the returns, vowing to take a celebratory drink every time I led a precinct. There were about 900 precincts in the city, and as the results began pouring in, I was leading in practically all of them.

Along about midnight Tony staggered in, solemn, long-faced, dejected.

"The election is lost," he mourned.

We were stunned, for apparently we had been leading. I shook Tony and asked him what he meant.

"You *can't* lead in any more precincts," he said in alcoholic tones. "The saloons are all closed now and we can't get no more drinks."

Election returns in those days were neither as precise nor as speedy as they are now. Before the days of television or even radio, the newspapers were the only source of "bulletins." They set up elaborate screens on the fronts of their buildings and flashed the latest returns upon them. We went back and forth from our headquarters to the papers, milling around in the crowd, trying to keep abreast of the returns. Then we hustled to the Board of Elections for the official tallies.

Standing before the huge screen at *The Cleveland Plain Dealer,* I heard people calling my name and I saw my picture flashed on the screen. The newspaper said I had been elected judge, but I was afraid to believe it. I hurried to the Board of Elections for official word. Finally at 3 a.m. one of the workers told me:

"You're in, and now you can get out of here. You led the entire ticket of twenty-eight candidates."

It was a great night. My friends and I went the rounds of our various homes to celebrate. There was my old friend, Judge George Baer, whose desk I had inherited in the prosecutor's office, and my old law partner, Joe Morganstern, and Louis Rich, the orchestra conductor. We kept it up until long after daylight, and by then Sam Silbert was a sorry sight. Still, tired and unshaven, I did not go home until I had visited the most prominent stationery store in town.

There I ordered a memorandum book from the clerk. When he brought it I stuck it under my arm and said, "Charge it."

"Charge it? To whom?" the clerk asked suspiciously. I told him.

"Judge Samuel H. Silbert?" the clerk repeated, mystified. "Municipal Court?"

"What's the matter with you fellows here?" I shouted. "Don't you take a minute to read the newspapers?" I stamped out furious, leaving the clerk to wonder whether he had lost a customer or met a judge.

There was a postscript to my first campaign. Sam Kest, one of my top campaigners and a very good friend, drove me around to most of the meetings in his Overland. On one occasion when we were in a hurry, Sam exceeded the fifteen-mile-an-hour speed limit and received a ticket. Sam, who was a lawyer, made sure that his case was held over until after the election; he also arranged that he should appear before me.

"Your Honor," he said, "I plead 'not guilty' and I have a witness who can testify to the fact that I was not exceeding the limit."

Gravely, I asked him who was his witness.

"You are, Your Honor," Sam answered.

"You are right," I answered. "I was a witness, and I happened to be looking at the speedometer before you were stopped. You were going twenty miles an hour. Guilty. One hundred dollars."

Sam, as I expected, did not have a hundred dollars with him, so he was locked up in jail.

And I, having had my fun, planned to send a bailiff down in a few minutes to have him released. But in the excitement of my first day, between hearing cases and receiving telegrams and personal congratulations, I forgot. When four o'clock came I left the courthouse to head for home.

On the way home I remembered my good friend and how I had shown him my thanks and appreciation. I rushed back to the jail and almost fell on my knees before Sam.

"Don't apologize, Judge," he said. "I got four cases out of it."

During the six-weeks period between election day and the date when new judges were inducted, a group of old friends in Newark invited me to a banquet in my honor. The dinner was held at the Progressive Club, which succeeded Jared Kimball's Newsboys' Lodging House as the official "club" of the newspaper boys. Hundreds of former newsboys attended the banquet, including three who were "sprung" for the evening from the Newark Workhouse. *The Newark News* placed a car and chauffeur at my disposal and *The New York Times* wrote an editorial referring to us as alumni of the "College of Hard Knocks"—a phrase that didn't sound like so much of a cliché back in 1915. Among the ex-newsies at the dinner were Morris Sheck, the toastmaster, who was head of his own advertising agency, and David Lynn, the vaudevillian, who entertained us. And, of course, my good friend Mike Hollander.

Many times in the last forty-eight years, I have taken the beautiful ivory and gold gavel I was given that night to court to use on a special occasion. I have never yet been able to wield it; it is much too precious.

CHAPTER 5

UNCHANGING THINGS: TAXES AND THE EXCUSES A JUDGE HEARS

MUNICIPAL COURT—my home away from home for the next nine years—had been started as an experiment. It was designed to replace the corrupt, ineffective Justice of the Peace shops. Supported by our civic agencies, the Municipal Court quickly proved to be a great improvement in the administration of justice.

As a prosecutor I had often appeared on behalf of the State of Ohio; now I was sitting on the bench, trying to decide who was guilty and who was not, in a vast variety of cases, both civil and criminal. It was infinitely more difficult.

Since "civil" and "criminal" cases are referred to frequently in this book, it might be helpful to have an easy, pragmatic way to distinguish between the two. In a criminal case, the suit is brought by the "State" with the district attorney—or state's attorney or police prosecutor—acting on behalf of the people. He is the *prosecutor;* the person charged with a crime against the state's laws is the *defendant.* Murder or armed robbery are two obvious criminal cases, but lesser violations of public law are also in this category.

A civil case is one fought out in court by two private parties. The *plaintiff* is the one who sues, the *defendant* the one sued. If any governmental body, such as a city or a school board, is involved in a civil suit, it is very likely to be so as the defendant. You might sue a school board for failing to provide transportation for your child, for example. On the other hand, the school board might sue a building contractor for having failed to comply with a contract. Traffic cases and accident claims are two major categories of civil cases.

During that noble experiment called Prohibition, our docket was crowded with liquor cases. Incidentally, it was exceedingly difficult to preserve the evidence in these cases, especially if the evidence was the real McCoy.

When I fined a woman $100 for illegally selling raisinjack, she burst into noisy sobs. Her husband clumsily tried to stem her bellowing by saying:

"Don't cry, Anna. In this country you must either pay taxes or fines. Come now, dear, pay your fine."

And in another case the defense lawyer pleaded, "My poor, unfortunate client has no money. To levy a fine on her would be unjust and cruel." You could almost swim in the tears that dripped from his eloquent voice. But his client, apparently, wasn't listening. As he orated she pulled up her dress, dug down into her stocking and extracted a roll of bills. When courtroom laughter caused the silver-tongued attorney to swing around to see what was happening, he broke off in the middle of a sentence, turned pinker than Sockeye salmon, and told me:

"Your Honor, I didn't know my client had this money. She has taken me completely by surprise."

I believed him. I'd been acquainted with the lawyer long enough to be sure that if he had known about those bills they would have been in his pocket, not in his client's stocking.

Traffic cases started to consume our time even before World War I, although obviously not to the extent they do nowadays. But even then the alibis for speeding, careless driving and illegal parking already sounded drearily alike.

One day a driver was brought before me for speeding. "What's your story?" I asked, bored.

"Judge," he said, "I know it's customary to have some sort of a tale, but I can't think of one. I wasn't racing to my grandmother's funeral. I wasn't on my way to a fire. I wasn't hurrying to get a doctor for my sick wife."

"Then what were you doing?"

"I was just speeding and the officer caught me."

"That's the most original response I've ever heard," I told him. "I'll have to fine you five dollars and costs for having committed the offense, but I hereby suspend sentence because of your honesty."

One morning at the height of an early-day crusade against careless speeding drivers—the fines I was dishing out were stiff indeed—I took a taxi to court. I was a little late and asked the driver to get me there as quickly as he could.

The cabbie nodded and started off, but I soon noticed that he had an odd way of driving. First he would glance carefully about, then put on a burst of speed, then slow down again and look back at me apologetically. The performance was repeated until we got to the courthouse. As I paid him he told me confidentially:

"I'm sorry I didn't get you here any sooner, but there's a son-of-a-bitch named Silbert on the traffic bench and I was afraid of getting caught."

I handed him my card and walked into the building without looking back.

Cars were harder to handle in those days, and although everything is relative, speed was becoming a mania. I sentenced serious offenders to the workhouse, hoping to slow them down in the future, and it generally worked. Flagrant offenders lost their licenses.

I also inaugurated a system which is still in common use. This was to impose a fine on a "sliding scale" basis. When we first put this into effect in Cleveland, the penalty was set at a dollar a mile for the first five miles above the speed limit (in this case above fifteen miles), two dollars per mile over twenty and three dollars per mile over twenty-five.

I never could stand listening to alibis for parking violations. Parking rules seemed to me to be plain. Either you parked properly or you didn't.

One such violator gave me the following story:

"Judge, I just jumped out of my car and jumped into

the post office. As I jumped back into my car there was an officer waiting for me with a ticket. I jumped back, amazed."

"Jump over to the clerk with one dollar," I told him. He jumped.

On my busiest day in Municipal Court I heard and disposed of 394 cases. It set a record at the time, but it was one I never want to equal again.

Although I had no use for traffic violators, I had even less tolerance for one of my colleagues, who indulged in his distorted sense of humor at the expense of the poor souls he was about to sentence to the workhouse or to a longer term in jail. When finding the culprit guilty on two or more charges, the judge would turn to his bailiff and ask, "Can you spell 'concurrent'?"

"No," replied the well-rehearsed bailiff, "but I can spell 'consecutive.'"

"Then make those sentences run consecutively," said the judge with a leer.

Ah, the excuses a judge would hear . . .

A woman was arrested for stealing bedsheets from a hotel. "I wanted to give them to my sister for her birthday." Thirty days.

A man was brought to court by an officer who complained that the culprit's breath smelled too "sweet." I'll say it did. He had swilled a bottle of lilac toilet water and got fragrantly drunk.

A woman was arrested for fortune telling. I offered her my palm. "Oh, Judge," she quavered. "I see thirty days in the workhouse. Please be more lenient."

"And ruin your reputation as a seer?" I asked.

A speeder asked me if I didn't remember him. "I was at a Kiwanis meeting only two weeks ago and listened to your entire speech." Case dismissed. That was punishment enough.

The lines of drunks seemed endless in those days before drinking was tabbed a social problem. One day I was startled to hear the clerk call out my name as a defendant. To my horror, an old drunken bum lurched to the bench.

"How dare you use my name on the police blotter?" I asked.

"Well, judge," he said, "when I get arrested the first man I think of is you."

Prohibition came upon us like a thief in the night. Here were some of its accomplishments:

People who never drank before became drunks.

Youngsters began carrying flasks—their declarations of independence.

Immorality, always shyly with us, blossomed out all over.

Prohibition became the nation's biggest racket.

Ordinary crooks became semi-respectable bootleggers or even quite respectable millionaires.

Cops formerly satisfied with a cool quaff at the saloon's back door could now accept big graft and play with big money.

I could go on and on, but others far more expert than I have dealt with Prohibition. Drinking, however, is a separate and serious problem, and there was a point when I tried setting up my own drink cure. It received considerable notoriety at the time. Known as the "Water Cure," it was a simple affair with no scientific basis. I don't believe it did any harm, and that is perhaps the best that can be said.

When a habitual drunkard came before me he was given a choice of spending thirty days in the workhouse or of drinking twenty glasses of water a day for thirty days. For a while our courthouse was lined with these poor souls, downing water as if it were nasty medicine. Still, for a month, at least, it kept the drinkers "dry."

Prostitution was with us before World War I, and it wasn't, strangely, as unpleasant a word then as it is today. At intervals it even enjoyed a quasi-legal status in most of our large cities and some of our "best citizens" approved of it. In Cleveland some of the buildings on the "line," as the street where the houses of prostitution were located was called, were owned by leading civic or church figures who assuaged their consciences by charging extremely high rents.

Now and then the community would break out in a rash of virtue and a crusading mayor and police chief would clamp the lid on the "line." But the crusade never lasted long. The ladies would be back in business, charging higher prices to make up for the fines they'd had to pay and for the lost trade.

Pimps acted as liaison between the women and police and were useful to the police as informers. The madames who ran the houses also preferred dealing with the pimps rather than with the girls, on the theory that the men were more "practical." A girl worked where her man told her to work.

Sadie was arrested many times for peddling her favors. An attractive blonde with zest for her work,

Sadie had only one gripe: married women of amateur status who played around with men-about-town.

"Since these gals started competition they're driving the professionals out of business," she'd say.

Sadie knew how to take care of herself in court when she was arrested: she simply demanded a jury trial. Quite likely some of her best customers were among the jurors. When women began serving as jurors however—alas, poor Sadie.

And then there was Rose, a determined young woman who was brought before me at least fifty times. She would pay her fine or serve her sentence and go right back to work. I admired her spunk if not her choice of a career: Rose achieved her ambition, which was to put a daughter through college.

My first six years as a Municipal Court judge raced by and in 1921 I found myself back before the electorate to give an accounting of my record and to ask them to re-elect me.

Again the field of candidates was extremely large so you can be sure I was as worried as before. But this time I wasn't a neophyte and in addition I was greatly aided by the endorsements of the Bar Association, the newspapers and important civic organizations. Nevertheless I campaigned night and day. Stalwart friends worked as hard as I did, among them Sammy Deutsch, Sam Kest and ever-faithful Joe Morgenstern.

For the second time I led the entire field of judicial candidates. I chose to interpret this as meaning the voters felt I had been serving the community effectively, and in 1924, when Judge John Dempsey ran for reelection as Chief Justice, I decided to run against him.

I was killed by kindness. Since there was nothing in my public career to be attacked, my opposition found a deadlier approach. I was ignored.

My friends were lulled into false security by the absence of attacks upon me and by my previous success. They were betting I would be elected at any odds. I didn't agree with them and, frankly concerned, I worked without let-up, going from ward to ward, precinct to precinct, meeting to meeting. But I was alone. "Why bother?" were the two words I heard most often. Then in the last few days it became apparent that most Clevelanders didn't know I was running. I lost. And then I collapsed from exhaustion and despair.

I was in bed for more than two months. All the battles for advancement, the campaigning for votes, the fights caught up with me. After two months in bed I was taken to Mt. Clemens, Michigan, for further rest and mineral baths and excellent care by Dr. Milton Smith.

For the first time in years I had time to sit back and re-evaluate my objectives in life. I berated myself for my impatience, for my ambitions, and for spending so much precious energy on some immediate achievement that I lost sight of more distant and valuable goals. And I decided one thing for sure. I'd never run myself to a frazzle like that again.

CHAPTER 6

"THAT THE TREE OF LIFE MAY ROOT DEEPLY"

THE CUYAHOGA County Court of Common Pleas serves the city of Cleveland and its swarm of suburbs. It is a busy court, manned by twenty-three judges. Civil as well as criminal cases are tried in Common Pleas, and suits can be instituted here for any amount, without limit. Some of the state's most important laws have originated in these courtrooms. And the court's reputation has been, in the main, unimpeachable. It is a court of original jurisdiction, with the injured parties entitled to appeal its decisions to the Court of Appeals and then to the Ohio Supreme Court.

In 1924, after I had returned to the Municipal Court, a two-year term opened on Common Pleas. I resolved to run. As a reporter put it in *The Cleveland News* some years later, "Sam led the ticket. He has always led it since."

In 1926, 1932, 1938, 1944, 1950 and 1956 I was re-elected to new terms as a Common Pleas judge; in my most recent campaign—1962—I received the largest number of votes ever given a contested judicial candidate in Ohio. My present term ends in 1968—at which time, Lord willing, I'll try again. At least no one will then be able to accuse me of being an inexperienced candidate.

All of this, of course, was a long way off and not at all in my thoughts when I first mounted the Common Pleas bench in 1924. One thing that did concern me somewhat then, frankly, was learning how to spit tobacco. My colleagues had told me that a talent for spitting was a sign of a first-class judge, and my competitive spirit would not let a challenge like that go past—despite the fact that I had never touched tobacco until then, let alone chewed it.

In our chambers each judge was furnished with a standard spitoon and, in addition, an eight-inch high, urn-shaped "gaboon." I practiced secretly until I achieved immense accuracy with this receptacle at twenty-four feet, and then I challenged and defeated the two Common Pleas champions, George Baer and Frederick Walther.

But I paid a price for my minor triumph. Before this I had, as I've said, never touched tobacco; now I found myself so addicted to the dreadful, delectable stuff that I was soon smoking twenty cigars a day. The only time, it seemed, that I did not have a cigar in my mouth was when I was in court, and then I chewed tobacco. I finally broke the habit by the so-called "reducing" system: each week, I reduced the number of cigars I smoked a day by one. I haven't smoked at all now for twelve years, but it was a struggle.

Until I conquered tobacco, it was a source of annoyance to my wife, to our hosts, and even to the press. John Vance mentioned my weakness for a "chaw" in the course of one newspaper column:

> Honorable Sam is no great hand for dignity. He prefers results. He loves to dive into tangled divorce matters, where both sides produce a stream of accomplished perjurers, and come up at the end with the answer in his teeth and everybody happy.

> As a campaigner the Honorable Sam is in a class by himself. He is the only figure in town equally welcome on the platforms of Republicans, Democrats, independents, mugwumps and what have you.

> Despite his record of uninterrupted triumph, the Honorable Sam is a prodigious worrier. At 11 p.m. election night the last time he ran he had a lead of 40,000 votes over the field. He was still frantically calling political writers at 3 a.m.

> Like all elected judges, the Honorable Sam would just as soon not get the hot cases, where great pressure is present. If he gets one, he takes it philosophically. The only thing to do then, he says, is to give it all you've got. This involves on occasion great mental anguish, assuaged by Sam's playing his violin. The anguish is thereby transferred to all others within range of the tortured catgut.

The Honorable Sam has grown constantly in reputation and ability, without sacrificing his habit
of chewing. He has grown as a judge, despite the
fact that he is still called Sam more often than
judge. I like him—but who doesn't? His full name
is Common Pleas Judge Samuel H. Silbert.

In 1954 my colleagues on the bench elected me Chief
Justice of our court system. Until 1962 I held that
post, serving with all the devotion and dedication
within me. However, as Chief Justice, I was not as
close to the people I love as when I sat on the bench
hearing trials, and so in 1963 I announced that I would
not accept re-election to the post of Chief Justice.

But sometimes you can have your cake and eat it,
too. Our Judges thereupon unanimously elected me
Chief Justice Emeritus for life; so now I have both the
honor and the title of Chief Justice and the satisfaction
of sitting on the bench as a "working" judge.

Incidentally, as frequently as possible, I sit not on
the raised bench but at a table down in the courtroom.
I find that by so doing I prevent histrionics. The lawyers speak instead of orating. The witnesses talk rather
than act. Dignity is not lessened—just as dignity is not
achieved by the mechanics of sitting at a somewhat
higher altitude.

Immediately after my election in 1924 I telephoned
my mother in California. "Ma," I shouted over the
buzz of the old long-distance lines, "I'm no longer in
the Police Court. I've been promoted! I'm a judge of
Common Pleas."

Her reaction touched and puzzled me. She sobbed—
a rare thing for my mother to do—and then assured me

of the faith she had always had in me. "You're a good boy," she assured me. "We'll always be proud of you no matter what."

But a few days later a brief letter arrived from her. "Dear Son, don't worry. I haven't told anybody. Not even your sisters."

I wrote back. What could she mean? She replied: "You were a Police Judge. Now you are a Common Police Judge. I will keep your secret. I will tell nobody."

Ma loved to correspond with her children. Undaunted by occasionally faulty English, she never resorted to dictionaries, preferring to spell phonetically. She wrote to us regularly.

A benevolent despot, she gently but firmly guided us this way and that. If we obeyed her implicitly, it was not as a duty, not begrudgingly, but because we loved her devotedly. It was slight enough payment for the debt we owed her.

Although my mother was only twenty-nine when she was left a widow, she never remarried. Until my brother and our two younger sisters were settled, she worked long, hard hours to keep her brood together.

And then, in the American way, we eventually scattered all over the country. I, of course, am in Cleveland. Ben became an engineer and has continued to live in Mexico. My two sisters are married, have families and live in Los Angeles. Mother, too, lived in that city in her last years.

Although she lived near my sisters, she maintained her own home. She felt that this was the way to happiness—each family its own entity. She never complained about life, and long after it was necessary she kept on doing her own cooking and immaculate house clean-ing.

My sisters visited Ma once a week; after they had chatted for a time Ma ordered them to go about their business and tend to the needs of their families.

I traveled west to visit her at least once a year. On one of those visits, I insisted that she go to a dentist for some repair work. Instead of arguing the point she took me to Griffith Park, where she pointed out the bears as they were being fed. She showed me how an old bear was managing to feed itself. It took bread thrown to it by the keeper, dunked it in water to soften it, and then ate it.

"See," Ma said, "bears are sensible. They learn to do things instinctively. They do not need dentists."

She loved to dramatize herself, loved holding the center of the stage when I arrived in California for one of our family reunions. She was the whole show—ex-cept that she would allow me to play the fiddle for her. As a violinist, my friends have always rated me a poor Jack Benny, but to Ma I was Heifetz.

She loved to sing the old Gay Nineties songs and could render "Little Old Lady Dressed in Blue" in grand style. She also loved to make speeches and liked to make up little poems. Once she sent a batch to Rabbi Abba Hillel Silver of Cleveland, who wrote her a letter complimenting her upon them. Proud? Those words of praise surpassed the Pulitzer Prize as far as she was concerned.

When I left home, Ma was living in Denver, where she had finally been able to buy a home with her meager savings. The place was destroyed by a flood, but instead of crying about her hard luck, Ma sold the lot, paid off the mortgage and started all over again.

When she moved to Los Angeles she bought a shack, sold it, bought another, sold it, and finally worked her way up to a decent home, where she kept herself independent by renting part of it.

I would send her checks regularly, but she'd never cash them. Not once. When I protested, she explained, "I'm saving them for my old age."

She still hadn't cashed them when she died in 1952 at the age of ninety-four.

Not long after I had become Chief Justice, I was invited to attend a constitutional meeting in Israel. Lawyers and judges from many parts of the world attended.

It was my first trip abroad. There was the excitement of the Inns of the Court in London, and the deeply moving experience of an audience with the Pope, arranged by my friend and fellow-Clevelander, Archbishop Edward F. Hoban (he was a spry eighty-five years old in June of '63). Perhaps most unforgettable was the contrast of the land on either side of an Israeli border. Green, fertile, alive with growth on the one side—lifeless, uncared for on the other. The soil was originally the same on both sides. The men and women and children of Israel gave life to their side; the hostile Arabians on the other thought more about invasion than irrigation.

I have been active with many groups during my life —with Catholics, Protestants and Jews, with whites and Negroes. In the Jewish community I have worked as honorary chairman of "Eternal Light" for the Jewish Theological Seminary, and for many years as a member of the Board; and I have tried to match, with my efforts, the dedication of B'nai Brith and its Anti-Defamation League. The sight of Israel's arid stretches being transformed into fertile fields now inspired me to work closely with the dedicated Jewish National Fund, and in 1961 I was given an unusual reward by this group. It was announced in a testimonial that read as follows:

TO JUDGE SAMUEL H. SILBERT:
Distinguished son of a distinguished people, we hail you as a great citizen of our beloved country, contributing nobly of the rich treasures of a penetrating mind, a warm heart, and a never-failing faith in the future of mankind, which God has conferred upon you in generous measure.

Lawyer, judge, teacher, you have been honored by the members of your profession, who have probed you most deeply, and by the people of this community, who have appraised your work. In the chosen field of your endeavors, you have served nobly in the tradition of the Biblical Judges who led, who counseled, who fought for the causes of the people.

Honored, too, by the community at large as Doctor of Laws and Doctor of Humanities; signally commended through the national recognition of your untiring effort to elevate the mounting problems of domestic relations in a disturbed world to a level of human understanding and compassion, you have retained a scintillating sense of humility and of humor which makes you an ever-delightful companion and ever-stimulating friend.

For all these contributions to the enrichment of life wherever you may be, we take delight in honoring you upon this occasion. Yet even more profoundly, we offer this tribute to you on behalf of the Jewish people of our community for your unflagging devotion to the prophetic idealism, the unfaltering vision, the steadfast courage of the People of the Book. In the councils of the Jewish National Fund and the rebuilding of Zion, your name is added to the illustrious roll of thoughtful and dedicated leaders who have wrought in our time the miracle of Israel restored.

We deem it fitting to honor you as you have honored us by planting in the Ohio Section of the Freedom Forest in Israel, a forest of ten thousand eternal trees bearing your name and that of your beloved wife, who has been your constant helpmate, with our hope that the tree of life may root deeply and grow eternally on the holy soil of Zion.

We inscribe this tribute with our prayer for many more years of continued productive leadership and happiness for you and Mrs. Silbert and with our thanks and appreciation for your long life among us.

This testimonial was inscribed at Cleveland, Ohio, on February 12, 1961, at the Annual Jewish National Fund Dinner at the Statler-Hilton Hotel, and was signed Julius B. Amber, president of the Jewish National Fund Council; and Suggs I. Garber, Leonard Ratner, Maurice Saltzman, and Max Simon, co-chairmen of the testimonial committee.

CHAPTER 7

A GUN IN ONE HAND, NITRO IN THE OTHER

AFTER A lifetime on the bench, it would be impossible to point to two, five or even a dozen cases and say, "These are the most memorable." Yet for various reasons, certain trials stick in the mind over the years. I hope that in sharing a few of these with you I can give you some taste of what it is like to be a judge.

No one who sat in my courtroom on a February afternoon in 1936 could ever forget the case of Clayton Clauson, on trial for armed robbery. For a few dreadful moments, it seemed unlikely that any of us would survive the trial.

Clauson was a giant of a man who started out as a youthful bootlegger back in the Prohibition era. He was arrested several times and sent to prison, where he received a broad education in higher criminology.

When I first met him in 1930 he had given up bootlegging for armed robbery. He was caught, and was subsequently sentenced by me to the Ohio Reformatory. There he proved so troublesome an inmate that he had to be transferred to the Ohio Penitentiary.

After serving several years, Clauson was freed to resume his career as a thief—this time with a new and deadly twist. In one pocket he carried a gun. In the other, a phial of nitroglycerin. Within eight weeks, the twenty-seven-year-old giant had staged a one-man crime wave of such dimensions that he had terrorized not only the merchants but even the police force.

His approach was simple; the well-dressed young man would go into a store, step up to the manager or the clerk, and say in a quiet, silky voice, "Sir, I'd like your money. I've got a gun in one pocket and nitroglycerin in the other."

And each time he'd walk out with the cash.

But Clauson got careless with his women, beginning to play around with more than one at a time. The inevitable happened: in a fit of jealousy, a bitter young woman tipped off the police to his next job. He was going to hold up the Sterling Hotel. Thus when Clauson approached the manager, he was seized by policemen before he could reach for either pocket. The cops took away his gun, but found the second pocket empty. Later, when he was more thoroughly searched they still could find no phial of nitro. Had he gotten rid of it? Or had it never existed? No one could tell.

Still defiant, Clauson told the officers, "I would have shot it out with you if I could've. But I'll live long enough to get even." They seemed to believe him.

In County Jail, as he awaited trial, Clauson grew still more bellicose. An honors graduate of Ohio Penitentiary, he put the fear of God into his fellow prisoners. And he kept boasting, "I'll go out feet first before I go back to the pen!"

It was strange. Not only the prisoners, but even the jailers and the deputy sheriffs had a premonition that here was one hoodlum who was doing something more than shooting off his mouth.

Judges have grapevines, too, just as do prisoners, and one of the things I heard was that Clauson aimed to blow up the court.

The atmosphere, admittedly, was tense when the trial began.

"Clauson," I told him, "I want to be fair with you. I sent you up once before. If you want another judge . . ."

"No, Sammy," he grinned, "you can try me anytime." Sammy!

It is typical of the big-shot robber that he is always broke when he gets to court. Clauson refused to allow me to appoint a defense lawyer, although he said he couldn't afford to hire one himself. And while I couldn't force a lawyer upon him, I still couldn't get rid of the feeling that he had a special reason for wanting to conduct his own defense. The grapevine kept telling me, "He swears he's going to blow up the courtroom."

Clauson had been built into a ten-day sensation by the newspapers, and the courtroom was packed for each session of the trial. He strutted like a peacock as he played counselor; and between sessions he boasted, terrorizing the turnkeys, talking about his skill with "nitro." The jailors established an extra guard and, as if that weren't enough, locked him behind three sets of iron bars.

I took precautions, too. I ordered that Clauson be disrobed in the anteroom and searched thoroughly before each court session. As he grew more and more arrogant, I assigned special deputies to each door. Detectives were stationed in the crowd.

And still, on the afternoon of February 20, 1936, it happened.

Clauson whispered across the trial table to the late John Mahon, then a county prosecutor, that he had something he wanted to tell "Sammy." Mahon let him walk up to the bench. (As his own lawyer, Clauson had freedom of movement—which, of course, proved to be his reason for having chosen to defend himself.)

As he neared me, Clauson dropped his handkerchief. He bent down to pick it up, dabbed it at his face, then crossed over suddenly to a detective, one of those who had arrested him. That placed him near the jury box. All this took place within seconds.

"All right," he yelled. "If you want to take me, come ahead . . . . and you'll all go to hell with me. I'll blow up every one of you bastards!" He held his hand high to show a small, amber bottle of fluid.

We were all horrified. There could be enough nitro in that phial to kill everyone in the room. Clauson raised the bottle over his head.

I think it was the women's screams that reached through to me. I rapped my gavel for order, though I was inwardly frantic. Abruptly I ordered the jury out of the room.

They were a mile ahead of me, and rightly so. But one poor woman suffered a fractured ankle and another ended up with a brain concussion. Spectators scrambled over each other for the exits.

Still I kept talking, trying to command an orderly exit, not even knowing what I was saying. And meanwhile Clauson stood there, hand high, eyes gleaming, ranting, boasting of the fact that he had outsmarted us and would "get" us.

Of a sudden the courtroom was cleared, leaving only the police officers, myself—and Clauson. The officers had their guns leveled at the robber and I was shouting at them not to shoot.

Then from the rear I felt a yank. My bailiff, John Sweeney—now a Divorce Court judge—had escaped into my chambers. From there he slowly opened the door behind my bench and reached for my chair, intending to jerk it, with me on it, through the door to safety. But John miscalculated the opening and I landed with a crash at the rear of the bench, legs, arms and robe flying. At the same moment all the guns in the room exploded.

A bullet hit Clauson's upstretched arm. Another slug ripped a finger off his right hand. A third went into his body.

The little amber glass bottle smashed to the floor. And nothing happened.

Detectives pounced on Clauson, pinning him down. He was bleeding, kicking and cursing.

"That dirty, double-crossing - - - -!" he screamed. "He told me it would be pure nitro!"

He was quieter when they put him on the stretcher. Yet when he spied the detective who had first arrested him, he could still bluster, "I'll live long enough to get you." And at City Hospital he summed it up: If he hadn't been double-crossed by that fellow who sold him the nitro, "Think of all the ambulances it would

have taken to haul all the dead people out of there!"
Then he added, "I would have had only one regret—
Sammy would have gone with all the rest."

Of course I had to dismiss the jury and declare a
mistrial. When he had recovered from his wounds and
was up for a second trial I again told him he could
have another judge. Clauson, with none of his former
belligerence, answered, "No, Sammy, you try me."

There were no dramatics. He got a long, long term.

Clauson never finished his sentence at Ohio Penitentiary. Not long after he went back behind bars he
smuggled a letter out to me in which he wrote how
sorry he was for all the trouble he had caused and how
hopeless was the life of the criminal. And then he said
he would be dead by the time I read the letter.

I phoned the prison warden at once. It was too late.
Clauson had managed to hang himself.

How had Clauson got the "nitro," in spite of all the
extraordinary precautions? It all seemed so simple,
once we found out. When he was arrested and
searched, the police didn't find any phial in his pockets
or on his body. But Clauson *did* have a phial on him,
in a tiny "pocket" sewn inside his trouser cuff. It was
never found, and that is the phial he relied upon in
court, when he once again was wearing his own
clothes. Ironically, it never was nitro in the first place.

CHAPTER 8

BLOODY BUS RIDE TO
EAST 105 STREET

WHEN THE noise of the gun had faded and the only sound was the empty clicking of the trigger, four people lay dead on the floor of the city bus. Blood seemed to be everywhere.

It was seconds before the numbed passengers finally realized that the slaughter was over. They surged forward to seize the man with the empty gun, Lawrence Goldsby.

It had all happened in twenty stunning, unbelievable seconds.

Or had it? Hadn't the stage been set for this carnage twenty-two years earlier? And almost a thousand miles from Cleveland—in Pine Bluffs, Arkansas, on the day when Lawrence Goldsby was born?

Lawrence's mother died when he was five; he never knew who his father was. When he was eight, the boy was forced into a homosexual relationship with an adult, an episode that psychiatrists later blamed to some extent for the fact that he became a homosexual himself. Young Goldsby had an I.Q. rating of "dull normal," and left school after the eighth grade. A brother was in an insane asylum.

A big fellow, Lawrence joined the Army when he was in his mid-teens, but was discharged when he was found to be too inept to carry out ordinary tasks. He became a wanderer with a minor, but growing, police record, jailed briefly in Cincinnati, Milwaukee, Chicago.

In April, 1952, Lawrence Goldsby journeyed to Cleveland to live with an uncle and a brother. He arrived unexpected and unannounced, and moved right in. He didn't look for work, but instead spent hours gazing at himself in the mirror, practicing pantomines with grimaces and gestures, counting cadence as they do when drilling in the Army.

Nights, Lawrence would hop in and out of bed; all night, in and out, cackling with laughter. Day and night he marched about the house, counting to himself, "Hut, two, three, four," wagging his head and mumbling to himself.

On May 12th, with sixty cents in his pocket, Lawrence decided to go to a movie.

He tried a neighborhood theater, but found that it didn't open until evening. He asked the policeman on the corner where he could find a movie open in the afternoon and was directed to East 105th Street and Euclid Avenue, one of the city's busiest intersections. There he could have his pick of shows.

So Lawrence got on a streetcar, made the short ride to Euclid Avenue, and then transferred to a Number

Six bus. A Negro, he sat down next to another colored man.

In the seat in front of him was Annabelle Frankie, an attractive twenty-four year old redhead. Goldsby stared at her hair, and then something—no one knows what—happened inside him. As the bus rolled along on Euclid, nearing East Seventy-Ninth Street, Lawrence struck a match as if about to light a cigarette, although smoking was prohibited on Cleveland's buses. Then he silently touched the flame to Miss Frankie's red hair.

The man sitting next to him quickly put out the flames with his hands. The smell of singed hair filled the air.

Goldsby became tense. He put his hands between his legs and muttered incoherently. Miss Frankie sat rigid, paralyzed with fear, never even turning around to see who had set fire to her hair. Nor did any of the passengers move, frozen, apparently, by the insaneness of the act. Only Mrs. Helen Harrison, who was sitting next to the terrified Miss Frankie, left her seat. She made her way up to the bus driver, a colored woman named Estelle Hill, and told her what had happened. Miss Hill weighed the strange situation and decided to drive on, making no more stops until reaching East 105th Street. There, she knew, a bus inspector of the Cleveland Transit System was stationed and policemen were always on duty.

It was a tense ride for Miss Hill and for the fifty passengers.

Finally Miss Hill reached East 105th Street. She called the inspector, Leslie Taub, through her window and explained what had happened. Taub summoned

Patrolman Eugene Stinchcomb, who was on traffic duty. It was 4:30 p.m. Traffic was heavy.

Patrolman Stinchcomb sat Lawrence down on a front seat of the bus while passengers began to get off. As Stinchcomb bent over to talk to him, Lawrence saw the service revolver in the policeman's exposed holster. He made a grab for it.

Stinchcomb tried to pin Goldsby's arms to his sides, but the younger man was a strong six-footer. He broke loose and shot Stinchcomb once in the stomach and once through the head. Next he shot and killed the red-haired Miss Frankie. Then he turned the gun on Mrs. Harrison. As he did so, a sixty-year-old lawyer named William Powers came lunging down the aisle in an effort to get off the bus. Goldsby thought Powers was coming at him and fired the fourth fatal shot. Then he swung the gun around again and aimed at bus inspector Taub. This time when he pulled the trigger there was only a clicking sound. The gun at last was empty.

The crowd grabbed for Goldsby and beat him until he was almost insensible before he could be hand-cuffed and taken to the nearby police station. Newsmen arrived and took his pictures. His face was puffed and bleeding.

Feelings between the white and Negro people of Cleveland ran high as a result of the multiple murder. The situation was so ticklish that any careless emotional spark might set off rioting, despite the fact that Cleveland had an outstanding reputation for understanding and co-operation between colored and white citizens. It was imperative, therefore, that the case be tried quickly.

From the beginning it was a problem to see that Goldsby—friendless, with no money and not much of a family, a man who had committed four senseless murders—would have a fair trial. I had difficulty securing good counsel for the defendant because of the viciousness of his crimes and because of the aroused state of the Cleveland community. Finally I was able to appoint, at the State's expense, Norman Minor, one of the city's leading Negro lawyers and a former assistant county prosecutor. As co-counsel I appointed Morris H. Wolf, a white lawyer.

It was a battle of psychiatrists from beginning to end.

First there was a sanity hearing to determine whether Goldsby should be committed to a mental institution immediately or whether he could stand trial. After this hearing he was declared sane and ordered to trial.

I ordered three psychiatrists to be hired on the defendant's behalf, experts on a par with the State's psychiatrists. They all examined Goldsby and their testimony became the key to the entire trial. If Goldsby were found insane by the jury, in spite of the pre-trial finding of sanity, he would be committed to an institution. If he were found sane, he could be sentenced to the electric chair or to the penitentiary for life.

The defense skillfully made much of Goldsby's weak I.Q., his loss of his mother, the sexual attack upon him as a boy, his own sexual peculiarities, his inability to cope with normal Army life, his babbling before mirrors, his cackling laughter. How could he know what he was doing?

And there was much legal haggling over the import

of Goldsby's explanations of the slayings when he first
was questioned by police:

"I shot the girl because she told on me for burning
her hair. . ."

"I shot the policeman because he pushed me. . ."

"I shot the other woman because she turned in the
alarm. . ."

"The other man must have been hit by a stray
bullet. . ."

"I was afraid, so I shot them all to get away."

Asked if anyone tried to assault him before he
started shooting, he said, "No. There was a vibration,
but no one assaulted me."

The State had its witnesses, its experts, who declared that Goldsby was legally sane—that he knew
the difference between right and wrong. And the State
made much of the fact that Goldsby knew enough to
kill only those persons he thought could harm him—
the policeman, the two women who had set in front of
him, the stranger who came charging down the aisle.

Carefully the State pointed out that the first thing
Goldsby asked one of the policemen after his arrest
was whether there was capital punishment in Ohio.
Didn't that prove that the man, the brutal killer of
four decent people who had done nothing more than
mind their own business or do their duty, knew what
it was all about?

The jury was as hopelessly confused as the experts
who testified at odds with each other. How, the jury
puzzled, could one set of doctors positively state that
the defendant was crazy when the other set of experts
could just as positively find him sane?

After long deliberation they found Goldsby guilty,

showing they believed him to be legally sane. But they
granted him mercy, revealing that they were not one
hundred per cent sure, giving themselves a little lee-
way in case they had made a mistake in judgment.
Who could blame them? Taking a life never righted a
wrong anyway, as far as I could ever determine.

And so the case ended without the additional
tragedy of a racial incident, as had been feared before
and during the trial.

I sentenced Goldsby to Ohio Penitentiary for life.
This meant that after twenty-five years a governor
could commute his sentence and make him eligible
for parole—if the Parole Board saw fit to grant his
freedom.

CHAPTER 9

ONE BOY, ONE ELECTRIC CHAIR – AND THE RULES

I WAS sitting one morning on the bench in Room One of our Civil Court when two lawyers hurried in with a most unusual petition. Room One is typically the scene of only the most routine sort of cases: the appointing of receiverships, the granting of temporary restraining orders, rulings on the technicalities in lawyers' pleadings, and so forth.

But these two lawyers burst in to petition me for an order restraining the warden of the Ohio Penitentiary at Columbus from executing one Emanuel Ross, who was to be electrocuted at nine o'clock that night.

Their request seemed to make no sense. I hadn't been the trial judge; I wasn't at the time even sitting on the criminal bench. And besides, only the Governor himself could issue a reprieve.

Ross had been properly tried under our rules of procedure. He had been found guilty by a jury, with no recommendation of mercy. The trial judge sentenced him to die in the electric chair. Ross's lawyers had appealed to higher courts and had lost. And now Ross was in the death cell, awaiting electrocution.

I asked the lawyers why they had not filed their motion with the trial judge. They told me he was out of town and that no one seemed to be able to find him.

They then had tried to get in touch with the Governor, they said, but his office reported that he was off fishing and could not be reached. It seemed obvious that these public officials had conveniently absented themselves for the day. In desperation, the lawyers said, they had come to my courtroom. They admitted that their move was unprecedented. Yet if I had the right to issue restraining orders in civil cases, why not in criminal cases?

While I could have dismissed their motion without even bothering to hear it, something within me would not permit it. I felt they were at least entitled to tell me about their case even though I didn't see how I could do anything for them.

This was their story. . .

Emanuel Ross was a seventeen-year-old, one of the "nobodies" of the world. In his short life he had merely been shifted and shuffled around in a cruel and colorless background. He had never been in any special trouble; the corner gangs he hung around with were harmless. He was legally competent, legally sane and legally capable of committing a crime.

One day Ross met a man by the name of King Young. Young, who was thirty-nine years old, took the boy under his wing and offered to show him a new, more exciting kind of life. As their "friendship" developed, Young told Ross he could help him see more of the world. But, of course that would take money. Young convinced the boy that the easiest way to get money was to wave a gun at someone and simply relieve him of his cash. As a matter of fact, Ross wouldn't even have to bother his head about getting a gun. It so happened that Young had one. And Young also just happened to know of a place that would be a pushover. They'd grab the money and start seeing more of the world.

Ross, who was not very smart, thought this all sounded good. Together they went into the grocery store Young had selected and attempted to part the proprietor from his day's earnings.

But something went wrong. Ross was inexperienced and nervous about games like this. So was the proprietor. The gun went off and the grocer was dead.

Ross and Young were quickly arrested and charged with murder in the first degree. They were given separate trials. The jury which tried King Young found the thirty-nine-year-old guilty, but recommended mercy. He was sentenced to the penitentiary for life.

Emanuel Ross was tried by another jury and defended by another lawyer. Even though he was only seventeen, and had never been in trouble before, the jury decided he should die.

As the lawyers came to the end of their recital I found myself aroused over what seemed to me one more case of injustice in our courts. Why should this boy die, even though his was the finger that pulled the trigger, when the older man, the hardened leader, was allowed to live?

But the processes of law had to be complied with.

The jury had spoken, and its voice was the voice of death. At seventeen, Ross would be the youngest boy yet executed by the State of Ohio.

I sat there frustrated. I could not see where I had the authority to intervene, and yet, if the lawyers were correct in their contentions, the boy would die before they could prove they were right. (They were proceeding on the technicality that Ross, as a minor, should have been brought to Juvenile Court before he could be placed on trial for murder in our Court of Common Pleas.)

But these were technicalities that should have been raised by Ross's original lawyers before he was brought to trial, or in the regular appeals to higher courts after the jury verdict.

Still, I couldn't abide the thought that through my inaction a boy would go to the electric chair because of a technicality or lack of precedent. I granted the injunction.

And what a hornet's nest that act aroused!

The lawyers immediately wired my decree to the warden at the penitentiary. Then one of them took the noon train to Columbus while the other drove. (The wire was sent so that the warden would know of my decree should they both arrive too late.)

Angry and dumbfounded by the turn of events, the warden stated that the execution would go forward at nine o'clock, regardless. I had no authority to intervene, he declared, and he would ignore my order even if the lawyers handed it to him personally. Yet while he stated this publicly, he privately called the attorney general of Ohio for his opinion. After all, the warden realized, a boy's life was at stake.

While the attorney general was studying the law, the Governor's secretary issued statements to the effect that the electrocution of Ross would go forward as scheduled unless I could show him a specific statute that would prove I had the authority to stop the execution.

I issued a statement, too. It said, "The State cannot electrocute Ross until my temporary restraining order is acted upon. That will not be heard until Monday. If Ross is electrocuted despite my restraining order, someone will have to answer for his death."

There the matter stood until minutes before the time of execution. The lawyers for Ross were in the warden's office holding a signed copy of my decree, when the phone rang. The warden talked a moment, hung up.

It was the Governor calling. Somehow or other word of the decree had turned up on his fishing line. He told the warden to ignore my decree, but to stay the execution. He was giving Ross a ten-day reprieve.

The attorney general, at the same time, found some law. He told the warden it was one of the most interesting tangles he had ever seen, but the warden could ignore my decree if he desired! However, he added, since the Governor had granted a reprieve, he would have to hold up the execution anyway.

I had taken quite a beating that day from our public officials, but the important thing was that Ross was still alive.

I wrote the Governor a letter stating my position. To this day I don't know whether he read it, but in it I said:

"It is the law's policy not to kill first and enquire

later, but to give the defendant every opportunity to have his rights defined. If there is any criticism of your action which permits a seventeen-year-old boy to have his fundamental rights determined before he becomes a corpse, I am ready and willing to assume all responsibility."

The judge who had presided at the Ross trial returned, and Ross's lawyers then filed a motion before him, on the ground that Ross was a juvenile at the time of the slaying and that the matter should have been brought first to Juvenile Court, entitling him to a new trial. (Incidentally, that judge was so angry at me that he didn't speak to me for more than ten years.)

The prosecutor's office, represented by a very capable assistant who later became a top criminal lawyer and now is a colleague of mine on the bench, objected that even if this were so Ross's lawyers waived this technicality by not raising the issue at the time of the trial. In other words, Ross should not be given the benefit of this technicality because of incompetence on the part of his counsel.

In the end the judge set a new date for the electrocution.

This time the electrocution did not come off as scheduled, not because of anything I did, but because the lawyers for Ross had appealed their motion to a higher court which ordered his execution stayed. The Governor had no other course but to acquiesce.

If I were writing a novel it would be possible to finish this story the way you would like it to end, with Ross's sentence being commuted to life imprisonment. But what really happened was that in time the higher courts over-ruled the legal technicalities. Further appeal to the Governor for clemency for this youth who had been voted to die, while the instigator of the crime lived on, was without success.

Emanuel Ross was electrocuted. He paid for his crime in full. Justice won out. Or did it?

CHAPTER 10

JUSTICE MEANS MOST WHEN IT MEANS FREEDOM

OF THE MANY satisfactions I have found in courtroom life, there is none to equal that of helping an innocent man go free. This is probably why Bob Carson's case is the one I like best to recall.

(Carson is not his real name. Let us permit him his anonymity; he deserves it.)

Bob was a "one-timer," convicted once for a crime. He had paid his debt to society, as we like to say, and had been released. He was not heard from again—until shortly after June 21, 1933.

At about eleven o'clock that night, a pharmacist and his clerk were closing their drug store, counting the money in the cash drawer, when three armed men entered. Quickly the intruders bound and gagged the druggist and clerk and pushed them into the rear room. They were just gathering up the money when a customer entered the store. A pistol was shoved at his side and he was ordered to the back room.

But the startled, frightened man stood frozen and the gunman knocked him over the head to the floor. A second thug grabbed his coat collar and pulled him out of sight behind the counter. Though it was late and the street was practically deserted, it happened that a pedestrian was on the sidewalk opposite the store just as the customer was hit on the head. Realizing that a holdup was in progress, the bystander ran to phone the police.

The precinct station was close by and the police arrived just as the robbers were leaving. One gunman was captured. The other two got away.

At Central Police Station the captive, who had a gun and $265 worth of pharmacy money in his pockets, gave his name but nothing more. That was enough, however, for the police to discover that he had recently been paroled from Ohio Reformatory after having served part of a term for robbery. Detectives further learned that the prisoner's older brother had also been sentenced to the reformatory for the same earlier robbery, and was similarly paroled. His description tallied with that given by the drug-store clerk of one of the robbers. He was found and arrested.

Hunting for the third gang member, detectives located the getaway car, an elderly Hupp sedan, parked near the drug store. The license plates had been issued to Bob Carson.

The officers raced to the listed address only to find it was a vacant lot. Either an error had been made in the records or, as was more likely, false information had been given deliberately when the plates were applied for.

But police are not easily discouraged and they began ringing doorbells in the vicinity of the vacant lot.

One of the householders said, "I know a man who owned a grocery in the next block and he had a boy named Bob."

"What did he look like?" a detective asked.

"Well, he was a tall, thin fellow with big shoulders. He wore a little mustache. He should be about twenty or twenty-five years old."

That fit the description of the third robber perfectly and the detectives had no trouble finding him; he was only a few streets away. They arrested him and turned over their evidence to the prosecutor.

Bob Carson protested all the time he was in jail, where his fiancee came to visit him daily. He was bitter, but felt sure he would be acquitted. After all, he knew and she knew that they were together at the time of the robbery, at her apartment, far from the scene where the crime took place.

The trial came before me on September 5, 1933. Bob was charged jointly with the two brothers for the drug store robbery.

The state presented witnesses who had seen the three robbers in the vicinity of the pharmacy. Each described the tall, thin man with the tiny mustache. Then the victims identified the same trio as the men who had entered the pharmacy. One by one they stepped forward to tap the two brothers and Carson and name them as the villians.

Carson and his girl used the money they had so painstakingly and lovingly saved to furnish a home, for an attorney. In vain the lawyer tried to force the older brother to admit that Carson was not the third accomplice. It was a futile effort since the man denied knowing anything at all about the robbery.

The younger brother did admit his guilt, since he was caught in the act, but that was all he would admit; he even refused to get on the stand to testify, as was his privilege.

Carson claimed that his car, used for the "getaway," must have been stolen. He admitted registering a false address, but said that was to evade bill collectors. However, his main defense to the jury was that he was elsewhere at the time of the robbery. His fiancée testified he was with her. She spoke slowly, distinctly and earnestly, striving hard to make the jurors believe in her sincerity. But they didn't believe her and when they returned a guilty verdict, it was against all three defendants.

I called the trio before the bench, to ask if they had anything to say.

Bob Carson was the only one to answer. "I'm innocent, Judge," he said. "I know I wasn't there."

I shook my head. The jury had spoken, and had returned the guilty verdict. There was nothing else to do but pronounce sentence.

"All three of you have been found guilty," I told them. "It is my duty to sentence you to serve from ten to twenty-five years in the State Penitentiary."

A short time after I had retired to my chambers my bailiff told me Carson's fiancee wanted to see me. Tears were streaming down her cheeks. "Bob is innocent," she sobbed. "I was telling the truth. I swear he was with me. He didn't help rob those people."

I had heard such protestations before, many times before, but there was a special kind of earnestness about this girl. I was as sympathetic as I could be under the circumstances.

"My hands are tied by the jury's verdict," I told her. "But if you can bring in new evidence—or find the guilty man—I promise I'll give your boy friend a new trial. See what you can do."

She went to the Detective Bureau, where she convinced one of the detectives to accompany her on a visit to the brothers. They talked to her about everything but the robbery. That, they wouldn't discuss. Frustrated, she came to me again.

By then I was convinced that Bob Carson was innocent. But it was one thing to believe it and another to amass evidence enough to upset a jury's verdict. I got busy with the Detective Bureau and we checked on one of the other lads who had been in on the earlier robbery with the brothers. We found him and questioned him. He denied that he had even seen the brothers since their release from the reformatory. Besides, he didn't have a mustache.

Yet when we dug further, we learned that he was lying. He had been running around with the brothers all of the time. What's more, he had worn a mustache at the time of the robbery but had since shaved it off.

When we were sure of our facts I ordered the man brought before me. I asked for Carson to be brought in, too, and I made them face each other. There was a sullen silence.

"You know you're guilty," I said flatly to our new suspect. "Do you want to let an innocent man go to prison?"

At last he raised his head. "No, I guess not. I'm the

one you want, all right." He pointed to Carson. "That man didn't have anything to do with it."

Naturally, I granted Carson a new trial, and a few days later he was free.

That is almost all there is to the story of Bob Carson, except that when they once again had saved enough money to furnish a little place, they were married in my courtroom.

I didn't perform the ceremony. I asked another judge to do that so that I would be free to give the bride in marriage, and also to serve as the best man.

CHAPTER 11

THE THREE TRIALS OF
THE DRUNKEN DRIVER

IF THE POOR man who stands before me in court has a right to expect a fair trial, so does the rich man. Yet sometimes we try so hard not to be influenced or prejudiced by a man's wealth, particularly when it is accompanied by position in the community, that we lean too far backwards. We may actually punish the wealthy man more severely than we would a less "fortunate" defendant.

One of the most difficult decisions I have ever had to make concerned the sentencing of a well-known, wealthy, previously law-abiding citizen who was the defendant in an automobile manslaughter case.

Before the night in question, Mr. K's name had appeared in the newspapers many times, but only in connection with civic or social functions. On this occasion, however, he and a female companion, out for a night on the town, had quite a few drinks. During the drive home there was an automobile accident; two men were killed and a woman was injured. Had Mr. K. been as anonymous a citizen as were his victims, the accident would have rated only a small story. As it was, the newspapers carried bold, black headlines—and the job of providing a fair, unprejudiced trial was thus made even more difficult.

Actually, Mr. K. had three trials all told. The first two resulted in hung juries; the third was in my courtroom. And the phrase "one law for the poor and another for the rich" was heard with annoying frequency.

In my instructions to the jurors I emphasized that they were to concern themselves only with the question of the defendant's innocence or guilt, and were not to consider what punishment a verdict of guilty might entail.

The jury, quite properly on the evidence, returned a verdict of "guilty." Now the burden of deciding what punishment was proper to the crime rested with the judge—and in this case the newspapers were loudly instructing me to extract the community's pound of flesh. As I said before, this was one of the most difficult decisions I was called upon to make, so perhaps you would be interested in my reasons for imposing an unusual sentence. Here, from my record of the case, is what I said:

. . . This defendant had been drinking—there can be no doubt on that question.

The jurors who convicted him, however, stated that he was not drunk nor even speeding, but that he was guilty of carelessness in his manner of driving.

The place in East Cleveland where the accident

occurred was poorly lighted. The situation has since been corrected by the city, which finally erected a permanent safety zone there. At the time of the accident, however, the place was poorly lighted and the defendant's visibility was undoubtedly partially affected by that situation.

The defendant has gone through three trials, each of which has been an ordeal in itself. A public trial is bound to cause humiliation, worry and anguish. While the amount of punishment inflicted by a trial cannot be accurately gauged, a trial is concededly a terrific strain on one's nervous system, and every defendant is undoubtedly greatly affected by such proceedings . . .

The defendant has made restitution. He has paid the afflicted families $48,500, out of which amount the sum of $28,500 came out of his own pocket, the balance from the insurance companies. To an extent, of course, he had a selfish purpose in view: he undoubtedly sought to impress the Court with his fairness . . . However, it must be ceded that he did a most unusual and commendable thing. It has been asserted that the defendant was wealthy. The court is assured that he broke himself financially in going through these trials and in his endeavor to make restitution.

This is the defendant's first offense. He has heretofore borne an unimpeachable record, and has led an unblemished life. He has worked his way from the ranks and has attained a high position in the business and social world. It is certain that he will never repeat the offense.

The defendant is fifty-four years of age. Imprisonment in the Penitentiary will not only personally disgrace him; it will ostracize and stigmatize his family as well. It will, in addition, likewise deprive the defendant of a pension for which he has striven these last twenty-eight years, and for which he has only two years to go.

The defendant is in extremely poor health. He is suffering from various afflictions. According to medical authorities, as announced by his counsel, his incarceration in the Penitentiary and the deprivation of special medical treatment which he requires would be tantamount to a death sentence.

Taking full cognizance of all these factors, and recognizing likewise, as the Court must, the effectiveness and the value of the probation system, the Court feels nevertheless that the offense committed by the defendant is too aggravated to pass by merely with probation. Punishment cannot be wholly psychological; it must likewise be concrete and objective, if it is to serve as a deterrent to the community.

Now this case has attracted wide attention and has been fully discussed in our public prints. Our newspapers are, of course, set up for the purpose of guarding the public interests, and it is fitting and proper that they fully and fearlessly discuss all matters of public concern. The Court can find no possible fault with the action they took in the matter. . . There is only one matter on which we have different viewpoints, and the Court wishes to state its position clearly on this difference.

It was pointed out that the defendant did not

plead guilty as he should have done, and that as a consequence he put the State to a great deal of trouble and expense in his three trials. It was not until he was found guilty that he conceded his guilt and pleaded for the Court's consideration. This criticism is entirely fair, and yet if we were to take the view that no one could get consideration unless he pleaded guilty at the very outset, we would be establishing a dangerous precedent. We would have a situation where even the innocent might be inclined to plead guilty as a way out, and where the guilty, in the hopes of receiving clemency from the Court, would be pleading guilty to gain favor. The Court feels that one cannot make a hard and fast rule in this regard. A person has the right to a trial, and simply because he has tried his case is no reason why consideration be refused him. If one merits consideration from the Court he should receive it, and that is true regardless of whether he has pleaded guilty when he had that opportunity.

As the Court has already stated, it believes that the sentence must be objective, and that while the Court has sought to save the defendant's pension, it had primarily in mind the benefit to be derived from this pension by the community. The Court mentions these matters by way of explanation in connection with the conditions that it is now about to impose upon the defendant. The conditions are as follows:

1. That the defendant serve six full months in the County Jail, where he is to be accorded the

same rights and privileges as are accorded to any other prisoner, no more and no less. . .

2. At the end of the six month's period he will be placed on probation for an additional five years from that date.

3. During the entire probationary period of five years the defendant shall not be privileged to drive an automobile.

4. During the entire probationary period he shall be required to report regularly to the Probation Department.

5. During the entire five years of his probation he shall pay to the crippled children of various denominations an amount equal to the pension he eventually will receive in a five-year period. The Court knows that his pension does not become effective until 1948, but the Court intends nevertheless that he shall pay an amount equal to the amount derived from the pension out of his pocket until the pension becomes effective, and thereafter his entire pension shall be diverted and assigned to the payment of the amount so specified until the payment has been made for five full years. It is the intention of this Court that upon every Christmas for five consecutive years as part of the penalty the Court has inflicted upon the defendant, that he pay over the sum of $2,475. to the Community Fund for distribution amongst the crippled children of various denominations and this amount shall be turned over whether it comes from his own pocket or the pension fund.

This was the punishment meted out to Mr. K., who had too many drinks one night, and then drove his car in such a way as to kill two men and to injure one woman seriously.

CHAPTER 12

THE MAN WHO JUST COULD NOT REMEMBER A FEW MILLION DOLLARS

ALTHOUGH NO man, as we have just said, should be penalized because he is rich, it has always seemed somewhat easier for me to be fair to the underprivileged. While I hold no grudge against the lord in the manor, I doubt if I could ever have sentenced Robin Hood. And when the man of wealth and power aggrandizes himself at the expense of those less fortunate than he, my every sensibility is outraged.

In 1933, with banks closing all across the country, it should not have come as such a surprise when the great Union Trust Company failed. Still, when any structure that has been an integral part of our lives crumbles, it is a shock.

To the Union depositors it was worse than that; and what was really unbelievable was the discovery that Kenyon Painter, the chairman of the board and one of the largest stockholders, had loaned himself several million dollars without going through the formalities of putting up collateral.

Although our banking laws in those days did not call this a crime, it was nevertheless the duty of the bank liquidator to find out where the money was and, if possible, to have it returned to the bank. But Painter wouldn't talk, and it was on the basis of this refusal that the incident became a case and landed in my courtroom.

Ordinarily this would have been the most routine sort of affair. I would have ordered the defendant to talk. If he refused he would have been sentenced to jail for contempt of court. And that would have been the end of it.

But Painter let it be known right away that he was no ordinary defendant. With his arrogant, overbearing manner, he took no pains to hide his contempt for the court and everyone in it. He made it clear that he had to answer to no one—and that most definitely included a five-foot-three immigrant named Sam even if he were a judge and in this instance the representative of 270,000 depositors of the Union Trust Company.

Not until Painter finally realized that a contempt of court citation was definitely possible, even for him, and that he actually might go to jail, did he decide to talk. Unfortunately, along with that decision he seemed to have developed a case of amnesia. He'd be glad to answer questions about the money, he said, but he simply couldn't remember anything about it. Perhaps he had misplaced it or mislaid it—he just didn't remember.

The bank liquidator gave Painter every opportunity

to refresh his memory; to no avail. Although the defendant could remember some details minutely, when it came to his assets, he was back to "I don't know" or "I don't remember."

When investigators went to his home they discovered that during the time that the investigation was going on many records had been removed from the jurisdiction of our court. At one time Painter said that his wife had many of these records. But alas, he didn't even know where his wife was.

It is important to remember that this was not a criminal case. The only power I had under the law was to sentence Painter to jail for contempt of court for wilfully failing to disclose his assets or for hiding them. But Painter said he wasn't hiding anything; he just couldn't remember.

The legal question, then, was this: Is it contempt of court to fail to remember? Can you be sentenced to jail because of a bad memory? Painter's lawyers said it was no crime. The lawyers for the bank liquidator, pointing to the 600-page record of testimony, liberally laced with "I don't know," "I don't remember," "My mind's a blank," and other such statements, claimed that it was perfectly obvious that the witness used these answers in a deliberate attempt to evade the real question of what happened to the depositors' money.

I had no precedent to guide me as to whether it was or was not a crime to have a "poor" memory. On the basis of what we had heard I decided that it was. Here is the way I put it at the time:

. . . The defendant takes the view that he is here under protest; that he owes no duty whatever to the Court, or the public, or the depositors, to explain any part of his conduct with reference to his finances. What he did say in that regard was practically forced out of him. He volunteered no information whatever, and in addition he put the plaintiff to considerable expense to obtain information which was within his possession and easily accessible.

Not only did Painter passively resist every effort made to obtain information from him, but he was actually guilty of many overt acts of concealment. In a former hearing he offered to prove that he was concealing nothing, and invited investigators to his home to satisfy his good faith. While these investigators were at his home, Painter was causing the records of all his transactions and dealings here to be moved out of his jurisdiction. In a former hearing he asserted clearly that he personally had no records, and that he knew no records were being kept by his wife. Now he admits that there are, and that there were, such records and that he knew about them at all times.

In addition to his records, which have been gradually and almost imperceptibly removed from this jurisdiction, the defendant almost managed to remove or hide all his assets. He was clever enough to perceive that reverses were coming and he got things out of the way. In addition to his assets, his wife and family have left this jurisdiction, and only the defendant remains to answer, if what he says may be deemed an answer.

Painter is truly a study in psychology. He claims at times to be suffering from lapse of memory. He appears nervous and uncertain, he is forced to qualify his answers with, 'I think,' and 'I believe,' and 'I don't recall.' He apparently is suffering from a loss of memory to such an extent that he cannot remember an occurrence ten minutes before, and is forced to have his memory refreshed by the record of the proceedings. Then again, he amazes us by the most remarkable display of memory. He is able to recall thirty-five or forty corporations in which he and his wife were interested; the amount owned by them in each, and the number of shares held by his wife and himself, and also where these stocks were purchased and were deposited as collateral. To borrow an expression from the attorney for the plaintiff, "Painter shifts from spot to spot, and place to place, like quicksilver." The moment he is caught with a new statement, he covers up with another. The truth of the matter is that Painter answers what is helpful to him and forgets conveniently what he desires to forget.

The court has said this before, and repeats that the issue is mainly one of honesty. Painter claims the depression has ruined him. If that were the situation, no one could blame him for not wanting to give up what he does not possess. The truth is, however, that he is not ruined financially. True, Painter may have lost something in the depression, like everyone else, but he has most of his assets and seeks to hold on to what he has. He does not act like an honest man, and does not put his cards on the table. If he, and his wife, and the others, would bring forth the records and honestly show the nature, extent, and character of the various trusts Painter established, it would be one thing, but when he interposes objections and maintains the attitude that he won't even give us his wife's address and tell us where she is so she may be served, it is a wholly different matter. The defendant deliberately keeps Mrs. Painter out of this jurisdiction because, as he puts it, she "resents" being interrogated about the matter, but his conduct and his motives do not deceive us in the least.

The Court has not a quarrel with Counsel, whose duty it is to defend Mr. Painter, but it resents the smugness, the complacency and the arrogance of this defendant. The Court dislikes making comparisons, but really, it has far more respect for a gambler who was recently before this Court for contempt and refused to answer on the ground it would incriminate him, than it has for this defendant. The gambler, at least, made no pretense of being anything other than what he is. He did not hide and seek to cover dishonesty and hypocracy by means of a cloak of respectability.

Dickens has talked of the law and its queer antics. And, in that connection, said "Law, thou art an ass." It is strange to see how a man who cannot account for over three million dollars can go free and make an ass of the law, whereas one who had obtained thirty dollars and would be up on aid and would answer as this defendant has answered, would be in jail ten times over for misconduct. I say the law is an ass if it will permit

Painter to get away with reprehensible conduct of the character he has displayed here and by means of twists and quirks avoid the consequences of THE Law.

The defendant does not like this Court, but that is wholly immaterial. He cannot choose his forum and must try his case wherever it is lawfully assigned. This Court, in turn, could have disposed of the case and gotten it out of the way by merely ruling on a question of law, but the Court felt it unfair to do so. It is required under circumstances like these to protect its dignity and its integrity. It cannot permit this defendant to carry on in this fashion and make a mockery of justice. The record, therefore, must be combed for fraud and possible perjury. These aid proceedings should be definitely pressed. The defendant must be pursued relentlessly and every possible legal remedy must be resorted to, so that justice be achieved.

Someone has said that justice is blind. Judges must be careful that by their conduct the public does not acquire the notion that they are dumb as well as blind.

The Court is not supposed to take judicial notice of anything. But they surely cannot be so naive as to believe that a man who has handled about ten million dollars very recently, should have no recollection of the most detailed matters, that he could do without books, checks, or records.

Painter may be sick; he probably is. He claims he is also broke. The arrogance of wealth, however, is apparent from his petulant and defiant attitude. . .

He deliberately tries to avoid perjury by answers such as "I don't remember" and by qualifying all other answers. He has been given a fair hearing and has had every chance to prove himself before the referee, and all that he has been able to definitely recall is the fact that he has had African fever. . .

Is he an honest man? He does not act like one. He claims he has no checks, no letters, no records. He has no files, no safety vaults, no anything; and mind you, he did not deal in nickels, but in millions. However, there is no dark mystery to me as to what became of his property. He made a trust to his wife, and to his children. . .

I will refuse to purge him and hold him in contempt of court.

I sentenced Painter to forty days in the County Jail and fined him $2,000. I was sorry that the law would not permit me to be more severe.

The lawyers for Painter never believed that he would have to serve his sentence. They filed their notice of appeal, and appeal they did, all the way to the highest court in our state, the Supreme Court of Ohio. I was upheld in both our Court of Appeals and the Supreme Court.

Painter went to jail, and the newspapers played the story all over their front pages. They carried large pictures of his palatial estate next to pictures of the cell where he would serve his sentence.

Then, after Painter had been in jail just fifteen days, his lawyers came back to me with a motion to free him. It seems that while in jail Painter had been reading the life of Cecil Rhodes, the British empire builder, who was described as a man who never kept any records and who was in the habit of making unintelligible business notes on odd scraps of stationery, newspapers and blotters.

Painter's lawyers now stated that Painter had a kind of hero worship for Rhodes and had patterned himself after him; hence the lack of records.

However, the lawyer for the liquidator of the bank, in opposing Painter's freedom, showed that some ten years previously, in another lawsuit, the banker had produced the most complete records that it had been anyone's good fortune to see.

In spite of a great deal of pressure, Painter served his sentence in full, and paid his fine in full. The legal principle that it is a crime to forget when you have a duty to remember was upheld.

Ironically, however, Painter never could be prosecuted for "borrowing" the money, or made to return it. Because he stuck to his claim that he didn't remember anything, even through a jail sentence, there was no proof that he had committed a crime.

As for the depositors, they all got their money back anyway. It seems that the bank really was solvent—it failed because all its assets were frozen. When the liquidator got through, there was enough money to pay everyone back at a rate of 110 per cent!

The Union Trust was reorganized. Now it is the Union Bank of Commerce, a giant in our city's financial world.

CHAPTER 13

A TALE FROM THE
LAKE ERIE DECAMERON

~~~~~~

A BURGLAR broke into the safe of a big Cleveland corporation and reportedly made off with $2,500. When he was arrested and brought to trial, his lawyer asked that bail be set at $2,500.

Since this was the sum reportedly stolen, the request was reasonable. However, the word reaching me on the judge's grapevine was that the criminal had really stolen $50,000, and that the officers of the burglarized corporation were withholding the correct amount for fear of trouble from the stockholders. Had I set the bail at $2,500, the culprit could have left the state with a profit of $47,500.

So I turned the lawyer down. Bail was set at $50,000.

Sometimes, however, even when you get a feeling that something about a case is not quite what it seems to be, you still can't do anything about it—at least not during the trial itself. One of the most unusual criminal trials in my courtroom was not even important enough to get into the newspapers. It was a tale out of Boccaccio, though, played on a Cleveland stage.

For obvious reasons I can't use the real name of this "criminal," so I will call him Gilmann. He was on trial for entering an inhabited dwelling during the night, a crime which could have subjected him to life imprisonment.

The facts seemed perfectly straightforward. The defendant had obviously entered another person's home through an open window in the wife's bedroom. The husband had entered the bedroom just in time to see the defendant exiting through the window.

In examining the room, the husband found a wallet with full identification papers. Police went to the address, questioned the man and arrested him. He didn't have much of an alibi. He was tried and found guilty.

I had no alternative but to sentence Gilmann to prison, even though my feeling during the trial was that the facts were much too perfect. When I sentenced him, he paled but said nothing.

Later, however, Gilmann had second thoughts and asked if he could talk to the judge. I arranged to see him and the true facts came out.

Gilmann, it seemed, was the lover of the woman whose home he had been accused of invading. Since she was married and her husband usually stayed home nights, she had arranged for them to have separate rooms. Fortunately for the lovers, the husband was not only agreeable to the idea of separate bedrooms, but was a sound sleeper and was innocently unaware of Gilmann's visits.

On the night in question, however, the husband

also decided to pay a visit to his wife's bedroom. By the time he had entered and made his way across the darkened bedroom, Gilmann was out the window. In his haste, he left behind his wallet.

The lovers determined to stay silent so that the husband would never know. But when the penitentiary became the only alternative, Gilmann decided to talk.

After hearing his story, I called in the woman, who confirmed it. Legal machinery was then quietly set in operation to give Gilmann his freedom.

I suppose the only moral to this story is that it stopped one man from philandering with a woman.

At least in her own home.

CHAPTER 14

AT LAST I TELL A SECRET CONFIDED BY DARROW

THE LATE Clarence Darrow once defined a criminal as a person who has committed a crime, who has been caught, and who has been punished.

There is very little I can add to that definition except to say that by our emphasis on punishment, as opposed to correction, we insure that our supply of criminals is constantly being replenished. No matter how we may pat ourselves on the back for letting prisoners play baseball or publish their own newspapers, our entire penal system is based on punishment —in spite of the fact that it has been shown time and time again that punishment never cured crime.

Furthermore, we punish on arbitrary grounds and with artificial limits. In Ohio, our legislature fixes the sentences—for arson it is ten years, for robbery ten to twenty-five years, and so on. How is it possible to determine the point at which an arsonist or a robber will suddenly see the light and reform? In our state a judge may send a criminal to a reformatory if he has not passed the age of twenty; if the conviction takes place the day he's twenty-one, he must go to the penitentiary.

Once, just before sentencing a defendant, I stopped to ask him his age. (Although he was guilty, there was something about him that made me want to give him every possible break.)

"Twenty-one, Your Honor," he replied.

I told him I was sorry, that if he had been under twenty-one I could have sent him to the reformatory instead of the penitentiary.

"But I won't be twenty-one for another month," he said quickly.

So I sentenced him to the reformatory. No doubt he was lying, but I didn't want to know it. It may have been wrong of me, and yet I slept better that night.

Similarly, we had a larceny statute that called any theft up to thirty-five dollars petit larceny, or a misdemeanor, and any theft over thirty-five dollars grand larceny, or a felony. Well, as you might imagine, there was once a thief who stole exactly thirty-five dollars and who was acquitted because there was no penalty under the law for a thirty-five dollar theft. (Although that loophole has been closed, the law that fixes the exact penny at which a misdemeanor becomes a felony is a ridiculous law.)

The difference of a penny or a day may affect the sentence that a man receives; so may a dozen other things, many of them having nothing to do with "law" or "justice" as we understand the terms. Think of the part that chance can play:

A man, for one reason or another, shoots another

man. If the bullet kills, he may be tried for murder. If it merely wounds, he cannot be held for murder but only for intent to kill or wound. If he is a really poor shot, he can only be held for assault. In other words, it is the result that counts most. Yet common sense would seem to say that the man in the third situation is as much a murderer as the one in the first, and that the first is no more a case of murder than the third.

In one case of bribery tried in our courts, two men—the briber and the bribed—asked for and received separate trials. In one courtroom, the man who was charged with bribery was found guilty. In the second room, on exactly the same evidence, the man who accepted the bribe was acquitted. Now it had to follow that if one was guilty, so was the other; if one was innocent, so was the other.

But two different juries, made up of two different sets of human beings, came to two different conclusions.

In another instance a jury convicted a defendant of manslaughter. The man's lawyer appealed and won him a new trial. This time, on the basis of exactly the same set of facts, the new jury concluded that the defendant was not guilty of manslaughter, but of first-degree murder! Instead of receiving a sentence of from one to twenty years, he was sentenced to life.

If a man *looks* like a crook, he'll have a harder time in any court, no matter how clever his lawyer, than will the man with the clean-cut open face. But the miscreant who goes on trial around Christmas often gets a break, no matter how guilty *he* is.

Chance, luck, or fate—whatever you want to call it that determines the age of the criminal, the exact sum he stole, the season of the year, the angle of his gun's inclination, the make-up of the jury—all these have not yet taken into account the ability of the lawyer or the nature of the judge. We have twenty-three judges in our Common Pleas Court with twenty-three sets of likes, dislikes, prejudices and attitudes toward interpreting the law.

The same case could be concluded differently because one judge abided by a technical, if ancient, rule of law, where a second judge might toss the rule aside. One judge may be severe, another lenient. One may believe in probation, another may not.

You may say that it is just to take these factors into account that we have higher courts to which to appeal, and to a certain extent this is true. But the element of chance operating in most of the examples I have given would not be cause for appeal.

I am not naive enough to believe that we can erase the existence of crime, but I do think we are doing just the opposite by our crude and ineffective treatment of the person who has violated the law. Like families who used to hide their undesirable relatives in the attic, we hide the undesirable members of our civic family in a nice, safe (meaning "escape-proof") jail, hoping, apparently, that on the date of their release, they will come out reformed and useful members of the group.

Once we had a police chief with a flair for publicity. He decided to give the city some direct action, to get rid of the criminal population all at once. So he rounded up all the known undesirables, put them in patrol wagons, took them to the city limits and dumped them on the other side of the line. The dumping ground he chose was the respectable suburb of

Lakewood, whose efficient police force promptly picked the hoodlums up and dumped them back in Cleveland.

The police chief got his publicity, but he didn't solve the problem of the unwanted criminals. In fact, by giving these men an additional reason for feeling unwanted by society, he probably made the situation worse.

Naturally, we lawyers, policemen, public officials and judges are not so crude in our methods. But so long as we equate imprisonment with correction, I doubt if we are any more effective.

Clarence Darrow, whose definition of a criminal is at the start of this chapter, was one of the greatest lawyers I ever knew. It was my privilege to call him a friend. I met him when he was chief defense lawyer in the Loeb-Leopold trial. I was sitting on the bench as an observer with Chief Justice John Caverly, the trial judge.

Only several years ago I was happy to be able to write to a parole board to add my name to the many who recommended a parole for Nathan Leopold, Jr., for I felt that he had paid his penance and would in the future be a good member of our society. You see, I practice what I preach, when I say that the purpose of our criminal law ought not be to punish, but to reform.

One night, while Darrow was visiting me at my home and we were reminiscing, he said to me: "Sam, would you like to know how I became a lawyer?"

"I know how," I said. "You passed the Bar examination."

"Of course," he replied, his sharp eyes twinkling like diamonds under a jeweler's light, "but the true tale is one that I'm not too proud of, and that I've never told anyone before, and probably won't repeat again."

Darrow had begun practicing law in the late 1880's. I knew from previous conversations that he had attended law school at the University of Michigan for a year, and that this was back in the days when study of the law was a two-year course. Thereafter he "read" law in a lawyer's office in Youngstown, as was the custom in Ohio in those days.

"Sam," he continued, smiling ever so slightly, "I don't think this will make the Bar associations too happy. So if you ever repeat this story, please wait until I'm gone and forgotten."

He's gone, but not forgotten, and never will be. Yet I'm sure he'll forgive me for finally telling the world how Clarence Darrow passed the Bar.

Darrow borrowed twenty dollars from some friends in Youngstown for the trip to Columbus, where, with a few other aspirants, he was to take his Bar examination on a Monday morning.

He arrived in Columbus on the Saturday evening before the test, checked into his hotel and, being gregarious, stopped in at a bar to have a drink. While drinking, he struck up a conversation with another gregarious fellow, and they talked and drank and drank and talked.

The next thing Darrow remembered was awaking in his hotel room. Sunlight was streaming through the window. His head was heavy and he could barely sit up. When he did, he noticed his drinking companion sleeping on the bed.

"Where am I?" Darrow muttered. "What day is this?"

The man in the bed roused himself, woke up groggily, and sat up staring at Darrow wordlessly.

Darrow got out of bed, stumbled to the door and looked out into the hall. To the first person who appeared he called out, "What day is this?" Upon hearing the answer he closed the door slowly, and without saying a word walked dejectedly to a chair and sat quietly, looking out of the window.

"What's the matter, son?" the stranger asked him. "You look as though you've lost the last friend in the world. Cheer up, my boy, you were brilliant—at least up until the time my mind became fuzzy."

"I'm brilliant, all right," replied Darrow. "I came down here to take the Bar examination on Monday, and here it is Tuesday. I've lost my chance to become a lawyer. I'm Clarence Darrow, the biggest sap in Ohio."

The stranger reached into his pocket, looked over a list of names on a sheet of paper, and said: "All is not lost, my boy. It appears that I am your Bar Examiner. Let me be the first to congratulate you. I hereby make you a lawyer in good standing in the State of Ohio."

CHAPTER 15

THREE MEN WHO FAILED A LEGAL TEST — AND DIED

~~~~~~

THREE TIMES in my life I have sentenced men to death, and never once did I feel that I was doing anything more constructive than to help society extract an eye for an eye. Certainly capital punishment never prevented a crime.

Centuries ago picking pockets was one of several hundred crimes punishable by death, and pickpockets were executed in public as a warning to others who might be inclined to so break the law. Great crowds gathered to watch the state claim its penalty; and as one thief was being hanged, a dozen others were practicing their light-fingered art among members of the audience.

Today we have statistics to prove that capital punishment does not deter murderers, no matter what certain police groups may say in its defense. Each year the number of homicides fluctuates between 7,000 and 8,000, with no correlation between this number and the number of executions. (Although only nine states had formally abolished the death penalty by mid-1963, in practice the sentence is imposed less often every year. In the Forties there were about 200 executions a year; in 1962 there were sixty-eight.) There is no evidence, either, that convicted murderers who are given life sentences instead of death are a threat either inside the prison or when paroled. Actually, "lifers" are in general the best-behaved prisoners. In my own state, of the six thousand convicts paroled since 1945, the group that has made the best adjustment has been the 169 first-degree murderers.

Still, as a judge doing my duty under the laws of the state of Ohio, I have sentenced men to die. Once in obedience to the findings of a jury, twice as one of a three-man panel actually meting out the death penalty. In Ohio, a man on trial for first-degree murder, punishable by death, may waive a jury trial. If he does, three judges are assigned to hear his case and a unanimous verdict is required for the death penalty. So although I am opposed to capital punishment, under our laws I am required not only to pronounce the sentence, but on occasion to vote for it as well if the facts so determine.

I had been sitting on the bench for more than a quarter of a century before I ever had occasion to sentence a man to death. His name was Edward Ralph, and he was tried by a panel of three judges.

Ralph's criminal record dated back to 1918 when, as a boy of ten, he was arrested for theft and sentenced to the Hudson Boys' Farm for a year. During the next ten years he was committed to the Boys' Industrial School at Lancaster three times for theft or incorrigibility.

It was late October, 1929, when the first of a series of twenty-five assaults upon women occurred—a series that culminated in murder. At a few minutes after ten in the evening, a thirty-four year old housewife, Mrs. Florence Alvins, was passing an empty lot near her home at Vineyard Avenue. The indistinct figure of a man appeared in front of her, grabbed her arm and whispered softly, "What's your hurry, baby? Gee you're pretty. Come with me."

Mrs. Alvins screamed and fought to free herself as she was pulled toward the lot. The man knocked her down. Somehow the struggling, shrieking woman managed to escape, but she was unable to give police a description of her attacker.

About three weeks later, twenty-two year old Hilda Kilmer had almost an identical experience. Upon hearing her cries for help, a neighbor called out, "What's going on there?" The attacker fled. Miss Kilmer could only say that he seemed young and short.

Three days later, another young woman, Esther Atkinson, had the same experience, although she was more severely beaten as the attacker grew more furiously violent.

These three were the lucky ones; they escaped. But within seven weeks, the list of known victims reached fifteen. To those who attempted to resist his assaults, the attacker became increasingly vicious. On December 19, Rose David was taken to the hospital after she was struck on the head with a piece of iron pipe.

Still, there was no real description of the man. All

that could be pieced together was that he was between twenty and twenty-five, short and shabbily dressed.

Then two women, in that week before Christmas, got a look at him. At midnight on December 20, Beatrice Gallagher was returning from a dance to the home of her employer, where she worked as a maid. A man stepped out of the bushes near the house and, warning her not to scream, began to pull her back toward the shrubbery. But Miss Gallagher screamed at the top of her voice, and struggled to get away. She saw the glinting of a nickel-plated pistol and heard a soft voice say, "I warned you," before she was shot, five times. Her employers heard the shots and ran outside to find their wounded maid lying on the grass. In the hospital, one bullet was found to have pierced a lung; the other four hit her arms and legs.

Two days later, Mrs. Mary Pschock, a young bride of three months, was accosted near Utica Avenue. She was shot twice, once in the back and once in her abdomen. Mrs. Pschock got a good look at the attacker; to the previous description she added the fact that he had a round, full face. Mrs. Pschock said, "I'll never forget it." Ballistics tests showed that both women had been shot with the same gun.

The year ended with no more incidents. Then on January 3, 1930, came the attack that aroused the entire city. This time the victim was a beautiful sixteen-year-old, Janet Blood—a senior in high school, an honor student, an only child whose mother had died two years before. When Janet tried to resist, the attacker shot her in the back. In the hospital she was able to add a few more details to the description of the man.

This latest vicious attack was one too many. The newspapers were demanding action, blasting the police for their failure to halt the wave of assaults. Inspector George Matowitz was put in active charge of the police department, and his first act was to cancel all furloughs and days off and to assign scores of men into plain-clothes for night street patrol. Next he picked ten policemen who, in high heels, lipstick and women's clothes, would act as bait for the attacker.

But instead the rapist assaulted an eighteen-year-old bride, threatening to kill her with his nickel-plated gun if she cried out. Weak and hysterical, she later could add little to his description except to confirm that it fit that of the man being sought. The next night another eighteen-year-old girl was accosted by the man, but managed to escape.

Meantime, Janet Blood was losing the fight for her life. On January 19, after sixteen days in the hospital, she died. Now the clamor in the city for the arrest of the attacker reached a frenzied pitch.

Harold Burton, who was later to become a United States Supreme Court Justice, had just taken office as Acting City Manager. He assumed personal command of the entire police department and put Lieutenant Frank Story in charge of the hunt for Janet Blood's killer.

Less than two weeks later, Edward Ralph was found.

Calmly, he denied everything; he appeared amused that anyone should suspect him. When Miss Gallagher and Mrs. Pschock, both recovered somewhat from their wounds and their experience, were brought in to identify him, Ralph put on a performance that left the police shaking their heads in bewilderment.

Inspecting his victims, coolly at first, a plaintive expression then crossed his face. "I'm terribly sorry I hurt you," he said to Miss Gallagher. "I didn't mean to cause you any pain." Turning to Mrs. Pschock, his tone took on an air of gentle rebuke, "You really shouldn't have screamed, you know." The two women definitely identified Ralph, who did not deny the attacks. "I don't know what got into me," he explained. "It must have been the liquor."

However, when questioned about the twenty-three other attacks, Ralph steadfastly denied that he was guilty of them all. "There couldn't have been that many," he objected.

And when it came to the night of the shooting of Janet Blood, Ralph had a detailed list of the drinking spots he had visited throughout the evening, and the people with whom he had spent his time. When asked why he knew so much about that particular night, he frankly said, "I thought I might be suspected when the girl died, so I went around and checked to make sure I was remembered."

While the persons and places on his list were on the shady side, the police were never able to break Ralph's alibi, nor was the prosecutor able to bring a murder charge that would stick. Although they were bitterly disappointed, it was decided that the best thing to do would be to try Ralph on the strongest charges available—attacks on Miss Gallagher and Mrs. Pschock. (It wasn't possible to try him for the entire series of assaults, particularly since the victims of his sexual attacks had asked to be excused from appearing in court.)

In the face of the evidence, Ralph pleaded guilty and was given the maximum sentence in each case, the two sentences to run consecutively. Which meant that he could possibly be kept in the penitentiary for forty years. Or let out in two, on parole.

With the arrest of Ralph, the frightful series of assaults was ended and Cleveland women once again felt safe on the streets.

Nearly two years passed. Then Edward Ralph was in the news again; he had escaped from the penitentiary. After three months of freedom, he was caught and returned, to remain there for about ten years. On January 27, 1941, Ralph was paroled.

In 1943, five-year-old Mary Jane Brady was raped, choked to death, and then tossed into a ravine behind her apartment. Eleven years had passed since Edward Ralph's crimes had shocked the city of Cleveland. By this time Frank Story had been promoted from Lieutenant to Inspector, and former Inspector Matowitz was now police chief.

When Story's men picked up the killer of little Mary Jane Brady, police found themselves face to face with Edward Ralph again.

This was the defendant who now stood in our courtroom asking for mercy. He had been arrested only two hours after having committed his crime. During this interim, while the young girl's widowed mother was searching frantically for her, Ralph actually looked into the mother's apartment and asked, "Have you found her yet?"

When the police arrested him, Ralph pleaded that

he was too drunk to know what he was doing. Since he did not deny his guilt, the only thing for the three judges to decide was the degree of guilt.

Ralph's lawyers tried to prove that he was guilty by reason of insanity, but this plea was over-ruled.

Once insanity was no longer an issue, the evidence as presented made a death sentence almost automatic. After hearing the testimony and examining the evidence, Judge Orr, Judge Day, and I retired to our chambers for deliberation. It took us forty minutes to reach a decision. The facts were clear, the guilt was evident, and the crime was so tragic that even the death penalty could not express society's sorrow, dismay and revulsion at the deed.

Ralph paled and trembled when I announced our decision. His hands were clenched, knuckles showing white, when he was led to the bench for sentencing. When I asked him if he had anything to say, he replied, "I told the truth, that's all." Then he began to sob violently. Recovering his composure, he turned to us and said: "Some day I hope to God you find out the way I have been treated in the jails and places I've been." Then his mood changed: "A man who would commit this crime deserves no mercy or sympathy."

Thus, having agreed to the verdict condemning him to die, he was led away to his cell, and soon thereafter Edward Ralph, a legally sane member of society, died in the electric chair.

Don Hagert. He committed an act of sodomy with a little boy. Then while the police were searching for him, he took a gun from his home, picked up a pair of five-year-old twins, and repeated the offense. This time, after satisfying his perverted lust, he killed the boys. Then he was arrested.

You can imagine the public indignation. Two innocent children's lives blotted out by a depraved adult.

What had society done with him or for him prior to the commission of these crimes?

The record showed that Don Hagert had been in and out of many mental institutions. It seemed to me to be axiomatic in those years before chemical therapies and psycho-therapeutic advance that the more crowded our mental institutions became, the more reasons were found to adjudge large numbers of the inmates "sane" or at least "harmless," and to let them out.

At the time of Hagert's trial the question of his sanity was the paramount issue. A special jury had been impaneled for a preliminary sanity hearing. After the panel heard much conflicting testimony, the youth was declared sane from a legal standpoint—in other words, he could recognize right from wrong. When the actual trial for murder finally took place, the verdict was guilty; the sentence, death in the electric chair.

This verdict was reversed, however, by our higher court on the ground that the jury which heard the murder case should also have been allowed to consider Hagert's sanity or insanity. The judge had refused to let them do so. A new trial was therefore granted, and this time the lawyers for the boy waived a jury trial. As presiding judge for the term in our Criminal Court, I appointed two of my colleagues to sit on the bench with me, as prescribed by law, to hear the case.

The prisoner loved all the publicity. He carefully

saved his newspaper clippings. He was sometimes arrogant, sometimes sullen, a boy of many moods. He enjoyed seeing his moods depicted "graphically" (I believe that's the favorite newspaper term) in the papers.

Once more we heard medical testimony as to his sanity or lack of it. We heard the evidence about the crime. When we retired to debate a verdict, our first chore was to decide the sanity issue. Under the rules and precedents we had to use as guides, the boy was legally sane, and once this fact was established in our minds we could not arrive at any other but the death penalty. Don Hagert, a legally sane member of society, died in the electric chair.

The woman testified in her son's defense: "I fell down a flight of stairs and landed right on him when he was just fifteen days old."

Her name was Evelyn Beach Kimball, and some of the spectators at the trial hissed as she testified. The crime had occurred on New Year's night, 1948. At 7:50 p.m. Sheila Ann left her East Side home in Cleveland to go to a neighborhood store.

Who was to know that Harold Alfred Beach, a short and chubby man with gold-rimmed glasses, was on the prowl, "looking for a woman," with a knife in his pocket?

Harold met Sheila Ann on the sidewalk, offered her a quarter, led her into an alley through a break in a wooden fence, then tried to force himself on her. She screamed and the knife plunged.

Sheila made it to a friend's house nearby, crawled

onto the porch. You could see the marks where her fingers clawed on the glass window beneath which they later found her.

The Cleveland Press and others offered rewards; a tip came in and Harold Beach was arrested in Baltimore. He apparently fled there because that was where his mother lived.

They brought Beach back to Cleveland, and soon he was on trial before me. It was another one of those cases where one battery of psychiatrists testified that he was insane, while another group insisted that he was sane.

He had spent some years in the Institution for Defective Delinquents at Naponock, New York, because of a sex crime committed against an eleven-year-old boy. In a relatively short time, however, New York psychiatrists approved his release because they were convinced, they said, that he was "not a dangerous individual," and because his father promised to give Harold a home and a job in his auto service business.

I played no major role in the trial, even though I was the judge who presided at the trial. The jury held that Beach knew right from wrong; on the very first ballot they agreed that he was guilty in the first degree. After three more ballots they reached the death verdict.

Weeping and praying, a legally sane man named Harold Alfred Beach died in the electric chair at Ohio Penitentiary on February 2, 1949.

The Beach case, incidentally, was an example of "trial by newspaper," where in its zeal to present all the news the press sometimes actually can commit an injustice. The papers tried Beach before he ever saw

a court or a judge. They not only found him guilty—
they even decided what his punishment should be.

Whether their judgment was right is not the point;
the fact remains that our laws say a man is presumed
innocent until found guilty by a jury and judge. The
newspapers should not take this great task of admin-
istering justice upon themselves, all for the price of an
edition.

When Beach was caught in Baltimore, a *Press* reporter flew there and obtained an interview with the
young man. The skilled reporter—Jack Small—and a
rewrite man, Dick McLaughlin, managed to get Beach
to answer whatever questions they posed.

There was nothing new for Beach to say when he
came before me on trial for his life.

James B. had dark, flashing eyes, a slim figure, and a
way with women. He was one of the most colorful
criminals I ever tried—and one of the least likely, I
would have said, ever to change his ways.

An energetic, ruthless gang leader, James partici-
pated in I-don't-know-how-many robberies before I
first met him; but somehow, no matter who else in the
gang was caught, James always managed to escape
arrest. Even on his wedding night he made his bride
wait while he went out to "earn" some money for a
honeymoon. His idea of fun was to pull out his gun
and shoot at his wife's heels. It was more than an
amusing sport; it helped remind her who was boss.

With this background, it may surprise you to learn
that James was all of nineteen years old when he was
brought before me charged with first-degree murder.
He and the Bell brothers, Angelo and Mike, had

planned an "easy" hold-up during a party at the Shaker
Heights home of Ray Dunham, a real estate man. But
from the beginning, nothing went as planned. It was
not part of the plot that the guests should fight back,
and this is where the trouble started. One of the Bell
brothers was knocked cold by a guest who hurled a
piece of lead pipe at him. The other brother was
tackled by a Princeton University senior, Ranson
Wilkinson. When Wilkinson appeared to be getting
the best of Bell, the thug yelled, "Let me go or I'll
kill you." Moments later Wilkinson lay wounded.

Meanwhile, James was running toward the car.
Thinking to aid his friends, he fired some shots toward
the scene of the scuffling. Instead he hit the second
Bell brother, fracturing his leg. When the police came
they found both Bells *hors de combat*. James had
escaped.

When Wilkinson died of his wounds, making the
crime first-degree murder, the Bells implicated James.
James claimed that he had spent the entire evening
with his dying father, but the police were unimpressed
and he was arrested and indicted for murder.

When James appeared in court without a lawyer, I
offered to appoint one for him at the state's expense.
First he growled that he would get his own lawyer;
then he changed his mind. However, when I named
Edward C. Stanton, a fine criminal lawyer who had
formerly been county prosecutor, James balked again.
(Maybe he didn't like the sound of those words,
county prosecutor.) At any rate, I finally appointed
Dan Cull, a former Common Pleas judge, and James
accepted him as his counsel.

Taking note of the caliber of the counsel I had

sought, the newspapers were commendatory. One editorial read, "James B. is an obscure person without political or social influence. It would not have been contrary to usage if the court had given the appointment to some young lawyer just going into business, or to some politically deserving mediocrity of the bar. Judge Silbert's action . . . will appeal to all citizens who regard human life as sacred, and justice as an important consideration."

The trial lasted more than two weeks, and it was an eventful one. Many of James' friends and fellow gang-members came to court; they frequently commented upon the proceedings, sometimes so loudly that they had to be ejected from the courtroom. Members of the jury were threatened and had to be closely guarded. One of the jurors became ill and had to be excused; his place was taken by the alternate juror.

In spite of all this, I considered that I had given James an impartial trial. When the jury of eight men and four women deliberated for five hours and returned with the verdict, "Guilty, with a recommendation of mercy," I asked him if he had anything to say.

He scowled and muttered, then stood up and said, "Yes, I don't think I've had a fair trial."

I was so angered at this that for a moment I was carried away, and when I sentenced him to life imprisonment I stated that he should be placed in solitary confinement upon arriving at the prison. However, I quickly repented and removed that feature of the sentence.

So James B., a wicked young man, was put away for life. Oddly enough, he turned out to be a model prisoner, so well behaved that he was soon made a trusty. He wrote to me frequently. After fifteen years the warden recommended that James be pardoned by the governor. As trial judge, I concurred. I felt, as did the others who investigated his case, that the fifteen years had served their purpose. James was released because his subsequent behavior was exemplary. He may be one of those statistics I quoted at the beginning of the chapter that show paroled murderers to be the best-adjusted ex-criminals.

As for me, he certainly justifies my belief that punishment is not the answer to crime. James and I have kept in touch over the years. Not long ago, when I was giving a post-election victory party, I got a call from him asking if he could come and help out as a waiter. He did a fine job. I am sure, though, that many of the guests would have been surprised to know who was serving them drinks.

CHAPTER 16

A FADED YELLOW CLIPPING
MAKES ME FEEL MIDDLE-AGED

WHEN I WAS a young lawyer I sometimes had trouble believing in the nobility of the concept of trial by jury. In those days our juries were frequently composed of beery, red-nosed individuals happy to dispense justice for the price of a drink. The basic requirement for jury duty—or for getting out of jury duty—was knowing the clerk.

On one occasion that I recall we actually would have been better off with the kind of juror who couldn't afford to buy his own drinks. It was during the holiday season. We were nearing the end of a second-degree murder trial, and had just come back from the noon recess. The defendant's lawyer was beginning to sum up, when suddenly one of the jurors got up and shouted, "I object!"

While it is routine for lawyers to object, this was the first time I had ever heard of a juror doing so. I asked the man the ground for his objections.

"On the grounds that I want the man to sit behind his lawyers instead of between them."

By this time I realized that our juror was intoxicated. I called a recess and questioned him. He admitted that he had been drinking during the noon recess, but when I threatened to jail him for contempt of court, he said, "Judge, you can't. It's all your fault."

"My fault? How do you figure that?"

"Well, Judge, if you hadn't given us so much time for lunch I wouldn't have had time to get drunk."

Some years later, well after the standards for jurymen were beginning to be set along stricter lines, we noticed that suddenly we were getting a wave of convictions in criminal cases. It wasn't the sameness of the verdicts that aroused our suspicions as much as the speed with which they were returned.

When we investigated, we discovered that every time the bailiff took the jury to its room he said, "Hurry up. You know the Judge thinks this guy is guilty as hell. Just make out your verdict and we'll get this over fast."

The headline on a tattered, yellow newspaper clipping says, "Women Jurors Have Made It Possible To Convict a Beautiful Woman, But They Don't Acquit Men Because They Are Handsome." And one of the subheads adds, "Even When It Is Necessary to Touch Up the Lips to Keep Up Appearances, the Woman Juror Does It With Her Mind On the Case Being Tried."

The story that follows is a period piece from the Twenties in a number of respects, including the fact that this earth-shaking report was permitted to run a leisurely 2,000-odd words. I think you'll like the post-suffrage flavor:

Women jurors give their job their undivided attention—says Judge Samuel H. Silbert—and then, too, women have stronger intuitions than men. "They sense things. They know when a person is lying and when he is telling the truth. They know when he contradicts himself, whether it is because he is confused or whether it is because he has forgotten his previous testimony." There is something about this that is quite unexplainable, except to say that women have stronger intuitions and more active consciences and do a better job of judging fairly than do men.

Since women have the vote it has been observed that it is the more intelligent class of women who go to the polls, while all classes of men cast their ballot, and this, of course, would raise the intelligence of the voters and thus the intelligence of those who serve on juries.

"Women are sincerely interested in the administration of justice," says the Judge. Being the mothers of the land they feel for the men and women who are on trial, but they feel also for their own offspring and they show a tendency to return verdicts that will protect humanity in general.

"They have proved, in this court at least, that they are not weeping willows, that they are not cold-blooded, stereotyped humans who think conviction is their job because they are selected to serve the government in a judicial capacity."

"What about the sex appeal? Does that enter in jury service, have you observed?" the Judge was asked.

"Bah! There's nothing to that," he replied as if he really meant it. "Women are not overcome by the handsomeness of the man on trial nor swayed by the charm of his personality. They see the other side of it. Women enjoy but are not carried away by the beauty of fairy tales. They always look for the sequel to the story."

"Do women jurors ever show their feelings in the courtroom for either defendant or plaintiff?"

"Not very often," the Judge replied.

"There are cases in court that would bring tears out of stone, and men and women have been known to be moved to tears by testimony and physical evidence of suffering brought into court, but I have known of instances where the evidence was such and the jury brought in a verdict not favoring the suffering one."

It was Judge Silbert who put forth the idea that a good-looking woman's chance in court was on a par with the homely one since women have come to the aid of the administration of justice.

"There was a time," said the Judge, knocking his pipe on the edge of his chair, "when a good-looking woman, especially if she were smartly dressed, could never be convicted. Men just couldn't make themselves send a woman to the penitentiary or to the electric chair. It wasn't a manly thing to do. But those days are gone forever. Women in the jury boxes know their sex too well and they know the tricks of the appeal to the man's heart and they discount it every time when it comes to giving judgment or verdict.

"They do not let sex sympathy enter into the verdict. Her good looks mean nothing to them. But they are fair, nevertheless, and they judge the case from the facts presented by the testimony of the witnesses. Their sensitive natures give them an understanding of things that men do not have."

"Well, Judge," said someone listening to the discourse, "does that go for all classes of women? Does that go for the timid housewife, the progressive, aggressive, energetic business woman, does it go for the clubwoman, too?"

"For women," answered the Judge, with a very peculiar kind of smile as if he were saying "Rosie O'Grady and the Colonel's Lady," etc., etc.

"Oh, I see," said the interrogator, as if there were still some doubt about the Judge's judgment in the matter.

"Whether a woman has been sheltered and coddled all her life or whether she has been bumping the bumps all her life does not change her or lessen her powers of intuition. They are inherent."

"Flappers, too? Can they also use this intuition advantageously in the courtroom?" continued the persistent questioner.

"Well, I'm not sure about my mental classification of a flapper. I don't know exactly where you draw the line between her and the more sober kind of woman. If you mean the snappy, bobbed-haired woman who uses rouge and lipstick and changes the color of her hair to suit her taste and togs every now and then, I think when you pin her down to duty you find her just as efficient, just as conscientious, just as interested and earnest on her job as the other type that wears the earmarks of constant concentration.

"I have observed that women take the business of judging someone else's court troubles very seriously and they are not nosey about it, either. My preference in juries is the mixed jury. The sound reasoning of men and the sympathetic and sensitive natures of women are an ideal combination. There you have a blending that is satisfactory to all concerned. I believe that in cases that are purely technical and apart from women's line of work she might not do so well in rendering a verdict. These are cases that she is unfamiliar with, the human element is not so dominant in them, they are too technical not only for women but for men who have not had experience along that particular line. But even then women have proved themselves to be fair.

"A few years ago the entire country scoffed at the idea of women voting. Now we have gotten over the novelty of seeing women at the polls and so will we get over the novelty of seeing them in jury boxes. It's one of the things that become a custom, and once a thing has become a custom the discussion and argument about it ceases."

"Can the fine sensibilities of women be roughed up by these experiences in Court?" the Judge was asked.

"That, I believe," answered the Judge, "is another old fogie idea. Women have fine sensibilities but they are made of stern stuff. They are not fragile creatures.

"I believe that women are big enough to know everything and keep their heads level just the same. I don't think they are spoiled by knowledge. They can fill their heads without getting dizzy and toppling over.

"They are fine and sympathetic, a little more sympathetic than men, but they don't squander their sympathy and they don't hoard it."

"Then you are not piqued about the women serving on juries, are you?" asked the questioner.

"Indeed not," said the Judge. "I am for women jurors. I am for the mixed jury because I believe the blending of masculine and feminine reasoning, sympathies and feelings brings forth fair verdicts."

And so forth.

CHAPTER 17

I DELIVER A CHARGE TO
YOU, A JUROR

As a judge I have sometimes found that the powerful hand of precedent, of doing only what's been done before, is as likely to result in injustice as in justice. Precedent is a tough opponent. And I have never found it tougher than in my attempts to bring about what I consider an important reform in the jury system—permission for the jurors to take notes in court.

Consider the operation of a trial. Upon its outcome may hinge a man's freedom, his reputation, or even his life. Hour after hour, day after day, sometimes even for month after month, the members of the jury sit in their box, listening to technical, complicated, sometimes irrelevant and always conflicting testimony. All of this they are later expected to sift and recall, accurately and impartially, before handing down a verdict. And yet, throughout the trial, the juror may not ask a question or jot down a note, even though to do so might help the ends of justice.

Meanwhile, counsel for both sides will take copious notes (in spite of the fact that, unlike the jury, they are already thoroughly familiar with the law in general and with the case in particular). As judge, I too have my pad before me. Only the juror, who will ultimately decide the case, must rely solely on his memory.

He will, of course, get help. Before he leaves the courtroom, I will instruct him on the application of the law to the particular case. But my charge, alas, will not be completely couched in laymen's terms. Part, much or all of it may be in legal language; the juror may not understand what I say, although another judge probably will. This, oddly enough, may not be wholly unintentional: we judges do not like to be reversed, if a case is appealed to a higher court, because of any technical misdemeanor on our parts.

If you have ever sat on a jury, you will know what I mean. If not, let me invite you to sit on a panel in one of my cases. We'll assume that you have received your summons, passed all the preliminary questionings by counsel, and have been duly sworn in.

Since this is an important case, the bailiff will escort you to your home, where you will pick up extra clothing and toilet articles; for the duration of the trial you will be confined to a hotel when you are not in court. I don't mean to be melodramatic, but this is the second time this case has come up for trial. After three weeks, the first jury had to be dismissed for attempted tampering.

The defendant has been indicted and charged with burning down a warehouse to collect $900,000 worth of insurance; therefore the case before us is one of arson. (Arson is the crime of burning down property and thereby obtaining illicit gain or money for yourself. Actually, it's quite a bit more technical than that, but you'll get that in my charge to you—or will you?)

The first thing we shall do is take you on an inspection trip, to the site of the burned warehouse. We'll all be along with you—judge, bailiffs, prosecutor and his staff, defense lawyers, perhaps even newspaper reporters and photographers. The opposing lawyers will try to impress you; it's all part of the game. By now, being human, you will begin to form impressions, to prefer one lawyer to the other. You may even, although none of us will admit it, form a prejudice for or against the accused. (And we won't admit either that anything you've read about the crime and the first trial in the newspapers has made any dent in your ability to be impartial.)

You still haven't heard a word of testimony, of course. So now let us go back to the courtroom, where your ordeal of listening will begin. You will learn (as if you didn't know it) that the defendant is an important politician, and that the crime in question happened *four years previously*. You won't be told the reasons for the delay. Therefore you may try to guess, which in itself will be meaningful in your ultimate decision.

In the beginning, according to the rules, we are going to make you think the defendant is guilty; in other words, it is the prosecutor's turn first.

The milkman who discovered the fire and phoned in the alarm takes the stand to tell you all about it.

He is followed by a fire lieutenant, who describes in technical detail the elaborate preparations that had been made to ignite 600 gallons of gasoline. He also describes the red-hot electric irons that ignited the trails of excelsior that led to the drums of gasoline. He tells you that a sprinkler system helped smother the fire in one part of the building.

More witnesses take the stand, and still more—all helping the prosecutor build his case. (The defense lawyer doesn't let them all pass unquestioned, however. Still, his real turn will come later.)

Now a most important witness for the State is sworn. A former partner of the defendant, he has already been convicted of the same crime and has turned State's witness. He will testify against his former partner. On the stand he describes buying the gasoline and the excelsior on the orders of the defendant. He tells of jamming the sprinkler system and he gives many details of his and his partner's participation in the crime —facts which presumably only a man on the "inside" would know. (Or so the prosecutor wants you to believe. The defense lawyer, rest assured, will try to prove that the man's testimony is nothing but the lies of a convicted man who has nothing to lose and everything to gain in turning State's witness.)

Next a brother of the State's witness takes the stand, and describes a conversation he had with the defendant during which, he claims, the defendant told him he was going to burn the building. The defense, when its turn comes, denies this flatly and vigorously.

Days have passed; testimony that you heard on the first day of the trial has been blurred or forgotten, but still you may not refresh your memory with a question or a note. However, it is probably safe to assume that at this point you lean toward finding the defendant guilty.

But at last it is the turn of the defense lawyer to prove that his client is innocent. In the following days, important civic and political figures in your city come to the aid of the accused. The lawyer for the defendant tries to show you that he had no financial interest in the building, and therefore nothing to gain by burning it down. (However, later a vice-president of a bank testifies that the accused was an official of the real estate holding company which held title to the property.) And so it goes, as two weeks pass.

Finally the defendant himself takes the stand. He accuses his former partner of lying and then states his case, earnestly and compellingly. You try to decide whether you believe him and his character witnesses, or whether you have been more convinced by the witnesses who have testified against him.

Finally, all the evidence is in, and I give each side two-and-a-half hours in which to sum up their arguments: to convince you why you should decide one way or the other. Each is persuasive and convincing, but you can only be convinced one way.

And now you will receive my charge to you. Luckily, since this is an important case, I have put my instructions in writing, and after you have listened to me you will be able to take a copy of what I say with you to the jury room for later reference. In the majority of cases, however, although my instructions would be just as technical and legalistic, you would have to rely on your memory of what I said. Since you probably won't understand what I am talking about anyway, maybe it doesn't really matter.

So this is what I shall say to you, the jury: (Those who are not dedicated courtroom buffs may want to skip the next 14 pages, and meet us at the verdict.)

This case was assigned to this Court for trial on June 11th.

We have been hearing it. Counsel having finished their argument, the case has now reached the stage where it becomes the duty of the Court to instruct you on the law, and to submit the same to you for your consideration and determination.

The Court has been requested to give you its charge of the law in writing. It will therefore read you its charge, which will accompany you to your jury room where you will be privileged to refer to it whenever you may feel impelled to do so.

The indictment in this case is predicated under Section 12433-1 of the Revised Statutes of Ohio, and charges that on or about November 30th, 1931, the defendant wilfully and maliciously, and with intent to defraud, committed arson by burning or causing to be burned, or by aiding or procuring the burning of the shop of the Blank Realty Company, a corporation, located in this county and state, contrary to the form of the statute in such cases made and provided and against the peace and dignity of the State of Ohio.

The defendant entered a plea of not guilty in which he denies all of the State's material allegations. With a plea of this character, the law places its shield of protection around him, and presumes him innocent until it is overcome by the State, by evidence, which convinces you of his guilt beyond the existence of a reasonable doubt.

All lawsuits resolve themselves into two parts; there are the questions of law and there are the questions of fact. The Judge is the sole judge of the question of law. Insofar as the law is concerned it is the duty of the Court to instruct the jury as to the law, and it is the duty of the jury to take the law from the Court and be guided by its instructions as to same, which it is required to follow implicitly. The jury, on the other hand, is the sole judge of the questions of facts. The jury takes the law from the Court and applies that law to the facts as the jury will find them.

You as jurors are made by the law the sole judges of the facts. It has not been the purpose of the Court to indicate in any manner its views on the facts—that is wholly your province. You have not the right to seek the bent of the Court's mind with respect to the facts, nor can you draw any references from what he might have said as to his recollection of the testimony. If he should have any views about the facts, these views are wholly immaterial and should be disregarded. The law has very properly made you jurors the sole judge of the facts. In reaching your conclusion on the facts you must be guided by your individual judgments, based solely on the evidence, and in the light of the law as given you by the Court, and upon no other considerations.

Not only are you jurors the sole judges of the facts, but you are also the sole judges of the weight and the credibility of their testimony. It is you who are required to weigh the testimony of the witnesses who testified here. You are not required to believe a statement of a witness merely because he has made that statement. You, in your discretion, have the right to believe, or to disbelieve, all, or any part, of a story related by a witness.

In considering the evidence and the weight which shall be given to same, the jury will very properly take into consideration the bias, the passion, and the prejudice of the witnesses, if any; the interest that the witnesses may have in the outcome of these proceedings, if any; the motives which prompted them to testify; the relationship that the witnesses may bear to the parties, if any; the influence these witnesses may be under and their demeanor upon the witness stand. The jury should also consider whether or not a witness is corroborated by other dependable evidence, or the admitted facts in the case. The jury must likewise consider the position of the witness to have dependable knowledge of the matters testified to, and whether or not he is a dependable reporter of the facts to which he has testified. The jury must also consider the reasonableness or the unreasonableness, the possibility or the impossibility, the probability or the improbability of the story related by that witness.

You will find the facts solely from the evidence. The indictment is not evidence. The purpose of the indictment is merely to apprise the defendant in writing of the nature of the charge against him.

Nor is evidence what counsel may have said to you either in their opening statements or in their closing arguments. The opening statements of the lawyers are intended as an outline of what each side was contending. The closing arguments of counsel were intended for the purpose of helping you to reach a fair and proper conclusion from the evidence which has been adduced before the jury. You will likewise disregard all repartee or exchanges across the table between counsel. Nor can you consider what was said by a witness and later withdrawn from your consideration. You likewise may not draw any inferences, either favorable or unfavorable, from any question which was asked a witness and which the Court refused to permit him to answer. Only such evidence as is material and germane to the issues is permitted in our courts. In determining the issues you will therefore consider only the evidence. The evidence consists solely of what the witnesses have been permitted to say, together with such exhibits as the Court has allowed in the case.

We have two kinds of evidence in lawsuits; direct evidence and circumstantial evidence. Direct or positive evidence is of a character wherein a witness has personal knowledge of the matters he has testified to. Circumstantial evidence means evidence of a character where the witness has no direct knowledge, but offers proof of such facts and circumstances from which a jury may infer other connected facts, which usually and reasonably follow according to our common experiences and which tend to show either the guilt or the innocence of the person charged with an offense. In a criminal case, the evidence may be either direct, or circumstantial, or it may be a combination of both direct and circumstantial evidence.

It is not always possible to ascertain the truth by direct testimony, hence the law permits circumstantial as well as direct testimony. Speaking of circumstantial evidence, it is not necessary that each circumstance standing alone be sufficient to warrant a conviction. If there be a number of different circumstances which, when taken together, cannot be explained on any reasonable hypothesis other than the defendant's guilt, and if in view of all of the circumstances, the jury is convinced beyond a reasonable doubt of the defendant's guilt, it would then be justified in returning a verdict of guilty. Where entire reliance for conviction is placed upon circumstantial evidence, all the facts and circumstances upon which the theory of guilt is based should be shown beyond the existence of a reasonable doubt. These circumstances when taken together must be so convincing as to be irreconcilable with the claim of innocence, and should admit of no reasonable hypothesis other than guilt. If the evidence be reconciled with the innocence of the accused, you should so reconcile it. Such proof, in other words, must exclude to a moral certainty every reasonable hypothesis other than that of guilt.

Expert testimony has been offered here in the testimony of the various individuals who were permitted to venture opinions. The rule as to such testimony is this: These witnesses are first examined in your presence to see if they are qualified; that is, if the Court will permit them to venture an opinion, they then may venture that opinion. You jurors, however, are the judges of what weight, credibility and importance is to be given to the opinion thus rendered.

The defendant has offered evidence as to his character and reputation in this community. The law gives him the privilege of offering this kind of testimony which goes to the jury, which determines its weight and its effect, in connection with all the other facts and circumstances of the case.

The fact that the defendant has been charged with a crime creates no presumption of guilt against him. The law presumes him innocent and this presumption of innocence remains with the defendant throughout the trial and throughout your consideration of the evidence, until it is overcome by evidence of the State. Not only is the defendant entitled to his presumption of innocence, but the defendant is not to be found guilty until the State has proved all the material facts contained in the indictment by evidence which convinces you of the defendant's guilt beyond the existence of a reasonable doubt.

Section 13442-3 defines Reasonable Doubt as follows:

It is not a mere possible doubt, because everything relating to human affairs or depending upon moral evidence is open to some possible or imaginary doubt. It is that state of the case which, after the entire comparison and consideration of all the evidence, leaves the minds of the jurors in that condition that they cannot say they feel an abiding conviction to a moral certainty of the truth of the charge.

A doubt is not reasonable if it rests upon or is founded upon a mere caprice, fancy, or conjecture; it is unreasonable also if it arises in the mind of the juror by reason of his own personal feelings, passion, or sentiment. A juror who acts upon such a doubt, or who creates a doubt in his own mind to avoid a disagreeable duty, violates his oath. A reasonable doubt is, therefore, an honest doubt whereby the minds of the jurors come into that state or condition that they cannot say they feel an abiding conviction to a moral certainty of truth of charges. If, after a careful and impartial consideration of all the evidence, you are satisfied beyond a reasonable doubt of the guilt of the defendant, you should then find him guilty. If, on the other hand, you do entertain an honest doubt, and you cannot say that you feel an abiding conviction to a moral certainty of truth of charge, then it is your duty to find him not guilty.

We come now to a consideration of the indictment. The indictment charges the defendant under section 12433-1 of the Revised Statutes. He is charged with wilfully and maliciously, or with intent to defraud, committing arson by burning or causing to be burned or by aiding or procuring the burning of the shop of the corporation located in this county and state.

In Common Law, arson was the malicious burning of the house of another. It had to be a human habitation. The value of the property was important in fixing the degree of the guilt. Section 12433, which has superseded the Common Law and now covers arson, broadens the crime by including the burning of property of himself or another; the value of the property burned is immaterial. So, too, the burning must be a dwelling or other buildings which are part of the curtilage or court. If the burning is of a property which is not part of the curtilage it comes under Section 12433-1.

You will observe that the charge in the indictment is in the alternative. It is charged that the defendant wilfully and maliciously or with intent to defraud, burned or caused to be burned, or procured the burning of said property. In the case at bar the State has not sought to show that the defendant burned the property in question. It has contended the burning was by others, but that he aided, abetted or procured the burning of the property by this other or others with whom he conspired in that regard.

Now to make a case under Section 12433-1, the State is required to show beyond the existence of a reasonable doubt these material facts: That there was a fire and that this fire was incendiary in its origin; that this fire occurred at the warehouse, which is located in the county and state. It is likewise required to show that the defendant, wilfully and maliciously or with intent to defraud, conspired with others, to cause the burning of said shop as charged in this indictment.

Evidence discloses that there was a fire and that burning took place in a part of the shop described in the indictment and that such fire and burning and part destruction of said building was incendiary in its origin. A fire was unlawfully started by someone. The question to be determined is whether the defendant aided, abetted, procured, or conspired with others to cause this fire, as charged in the indictment.

The word "maliciously" as used in this section, means an act done without just or legal excuse and done from a wrong motive with intent to injure another; this design may be prompted by deliberate hatred, or revenge, or by the hope or desire for gain or reward. In the ordinary acceptance of the term, malice means hatred, or ill will, but in a legal sense it is not necessary that such a fact appear if what was done springs from a wantonness or depravity of the heart by a person bent upon mischief.

"Wilfully" means anything done intentionally; it may be said to be a state of mind importing a will, intention, or design to do an act. The presence of wilfullness or purpose is a question of fact to be determined from all the facts and circumstances of the case. We have ordinarily no power of reading a person's mind, as to whether what was done was wilful. We are required to infer it, more or less satisfactorily, from his acts. Hence a person is presumed to intend to be conscious of what he or she in fact does.

Section 12380 provides as follows:

Whoever aids, abets, or procures another to commit an offense may be prosecuted as if he were the principal offender.

Before you can convict the defendant as an aider and abettor, you must find from the evidence that the defendant actually aided and abetted or procured another or others to burn the building in question. The causing of the burning of the building by persons charged by the State with having burned them at the instance of the defendant, must be proved by evidence adduced at the trial. Mere suspicions or conjectures in that regard are not sufficient to take the place of such evidence. Such evidence of a burning of the premises by those who are aided, abetted or procured to do the act by the defendant must be of a character to convince you beyond a reasonable doubt. If another or others did the manual act of burning the shop and if it was done in pursuance to a common design or purpose of the defendant, and at his instance and instigation, he would be guilty under this Section of the statutes.

Aid means to help or assist or strengthen; abet means to encourage, counsel, incite or assist. Procure means to produce, to bring about, or cause the bringing about of an act.

A conspiracy in law is the formulation between the two or more persons of a plan or scheme to do an unlawful act. It is a combination by concerted action on the part of those concerned to accomplish some criminal or unlawful purpose. If and when a conspiracy has been established by the evidence as existing between two or more persons, then the acts of one become the acts of the other or others joined in such conspiracy, whether such conspiracy or such act was performed in or out, without or away from the presence of the other or others joined in such plan or scheme to perform an unlawful act. Whether a conspiracy in fact existed in this case is a question of fact for the jury. To warrant the jury in finding there was a conspiracy it is not necessary that there be evidence that expressly shows that to be the situation. It is essential, however, that there be shown to have been a common design between the parties charged with having formed the conspiracy to warrant you in finding that a conspiracy in fact existed. It is not necessary that the defendant here with others charged with having formed such a conspiracy come together and actually agree in terms to have acted in common design. If it should appear that the defendant with others alleged to have proceeded in a common design, pursued by their acts the same objective, and by the same means, the one performing one part and another, another part of the same, so as to complete it with a view or purpose of obtainment or consummation of the same object or end, the jury may consider such evidence, if any such evidence there be, to determine whether the defendant and others were or were not engaged in a conspiracy to effect the object of such a conspiracy.

Now a word on the question of motive or absence of motives on the part of the defendant. The legal title to the premises in question was in the name of a corporation at the time of the fire.

There had been a bond issue placed on said property secured by a mortgage deed. The corporation defaulted upon the payments of interest and principal on the bonds. In the month of August, 1931, the corporation transferred in writing the possession, management and rents to a trustee for the bondholders. Shortly thereafter a foreclosure was filed against the corporation by the trustee for the bondholders in the Federal Court, which action was pending at the time of the alleged burning of the property. The company's equity was therefore not foreclosed until the filing of the decree which took place in February of 1932. The possession, control, and management of the property was out of the corporation at the time of the fire, but it still retained the title and was the owner of the aforesaid property.

The defendant contends that he was sold out in the stock-market crash of 1924-30; that this sale included all his stocks as well as his stock in this corporation, and that he, therefore, had no financial interest in the premises thereafter regardless of whose name the stock stood in. The State contends in that regard that the stock was merely delivered to accounts receivable, but that he was not actually sold out as he contends. The jury has the right in this regard to consider the motive or lack of motive on the part of the defendant. Could the defendant profit by a fire? Did he have a motive for committing same or aiding in its commission? This question as to whether there was a motive or a lack of motive should be considered by the jury. The State is not required to prove motive to convict the defendant, but if there was in fact no motive for the crime then that circumstance should be considered by the jury in determining whether the defendant did commit the crime.

When you get to your jury room, the first thing you will do will be to choose a foreman or forelady and then you will proceed to deliberate in an orderly manner until you reach a verdict. You will have with you two forms of verdict, one being a verdict of guilty, and the other being a verdict of not guilty. Being guided by the evidence under the instructions of the law as given you, should you find that the State has failed to establish the guilt of this defendant, as charged in this indictment, then it will be your duty to find him not guilty and you will so indicate by returning that form of verdict. If the State, however, has established his guilt, then you will find him guilty and so indicate by returning the other form of verdict.

There is one more fact that should be noted in a criminal trial. You are required to unanimously concur in that verdict.

The Court's task in this case is now completed. It has endeavored to conduct this hearing impartially and to present the issues to you fairly. Your task is about to begin. In considering this case you are to give it your individual consideration and judgment and you are to base the same on the evidence and under the rules of law as the Court has given them to you, which rules are binding upon the individual conscience and judgment of this panel. It is the duty of the jurors while deliberating over their verdict to confer with their fellow jurors and give consideration to their views in an effort to arrive at a common conclusion, and to that end you should deliberate. You must exclude from your minds all impressions which you may have fathered consciously or unconsciously, and come to your conclusion solely on the merits of the case. You must disregard all passion, prejudice, and sympathy; you should permit none of these to influence your minds. So, too, it should be stated that you have nothing whatever to do with consequences of your verdict. The question of punishment is wholly in the province of the Court. You should look only to the law and the facts in reaching a conclusion.

Now you have been drafted for service in this case. You have been separated from your families and your social activities for a considerable length of time. Some of you have even made great financial sacrifices. The Court would not blame you if you are somewhat resentful. Nevertheless, the Court felt it his duty to segregate you. Neither side should be blamed for this. The Court desires to thank you individually and collectively for your public spirit and the service you have rendered.

In conclusion I will say that you must enforce the law fearlessly. You would be faithless to your trust if you returned a verdict of acquittal when the facts demand conviction of the defendant. It is fully as important that the innocent be not punished. You are impaneled not for vengeance, but to subserve the ends of public justice. You would be disloyal to your obligations if you should find the defendant guilty when evidence requires his acquittal. Your verdict must be honest, intelligent and in conformity with the evidence.

You may now take the case. The thirteenth juror will be excused with the thanks of the Court.

There is your case, and there is my charge. Imagine how much of it you would remember were you unable to refer to it during your deliberations. (And how much of it do you really understand, by the way?) However, you are more fortunate than most juries: you have a written document to which to refer. Furthermore, this is a relatively simple criminal case. Still, you have much to decide: You must know the difference between reasonable doubt and guilt beyond reasonable doubt; you must understand the exact significance of aiding and abetting; and you must know what to exclude from your mind every time the judge sustained an objection. Will you remember all that? And do you really think you can "exclude" something from your mind just because I tell you to?

Now, then, what is your verdict?

The jury in this particular case found the defendant not guilty.

One day, when I was presiding at the Criminal Court, a juror suddenly interrupted the proceedings to ask a question of the witness on the stand. The lawyers were shocked. I called them to the bench and talked to them, and we all agreed to permit the questions without objection. We tried it several times thereafter and we got along quite well because neither side took objections.

When I returned to the civil branch of our Court

I began to notice that the jurors frequently took notes surreptitiously. Since the lawyers also noticed it, but said nothing, I kept silent about the matter. Finally, I felt that it was about time for the matter to be brought into the open. I took the initiative, and put my thoughts into action.

The case of Corbin vs. the City of Cleveland was assigned to my courtroom for trial. A simple personal injury suit brought by a person who had stepped into a hole in the sidewalk and was suing the City, it was one of hundreds of cases, all similar in nature, that are filed against a municipality each year. It would have been just another routine case in the legal annals of our Court if the case had been tried in a routine manner.

But in this instance, after a jury had been impaneled and sworn in, I suggested, without the request of either litigant and actually over their objections, that the jurors might take notes on the evidence presented. The Court would furnish them with the necessary materials and instruct them as to how they should be kept during the progress of the trial. In fact, here is the exact language I used in talking to that jury:

> I am permitting the jurors to take notes. I am handing each juror an envelope with some blank paper inside. If a juror wants to write down a note or two as the lawyers or the parties talk, he has a right to do so. At the end of the day I want the jurors to seal up their own envelopes, write their names across the sealed parts and hand them to the Court. In the morning, I will return each envelope to the juror who gave it to me, unopened,

and the jurors can take these notes into their jury room if they wish. After the case is completed, the notes will have to be destroyed. Nobody will be permitted to see your notes. So I hand one of these to each of you, and either side may take an exception if they desire to do so.

You do not have to take notes unless you desire to do so, but if you desire to, you can take whatever notes you wish, seal them up so nobody sees your notes, and in the morning you will be handed back your sealed envelope. At the conclusion of the entire case you will return your notes to me and they will be destroyed in your presence.

The jury awarded their judgment for the defendant. The plaintiff appealed to the Court of Appeals which granted him a new trial because I had allowed the jurors to take notes. The higher court held that I had committed prejudicial error in encouraging the jurors to take notes over the objections of both parties.

The case then went to the Supreme Court of Ohio which sustained the reversal, saying that some jurors, incompetent to take notes, might nevertheless have taken them under the mistaken belief that it was their duty to do so.

Repudiated in my efforts by both our Court of Appeals and the Supreme Court, I took the matter up with the State Bar Association. Actually, I had done so once before, but the matter had been referred to a committee, where presumably it died. This second time, however, with the Corbin Case already decided, there was no reason for the committee not to act.

Now the tables were reversed and I was pleading

a case before lawyers. To my plea for note taking, I
also added the right of a juror to ask any question in
his mind, through the court, with the proper safe-
guards. After all, if the ends of justice are to be served,
they will be served best by leaving as little as possible
to the realm of conjecture.

I told the committee:

"You must remember that in the old days the facts
presented to jurors were simple. Most of the cases were
trivial—suits over whether a fence encroached on another man's property and the like.

"Today many very complicated questions are
brought into our courts. If our courts are to operate
smoothly and efficiently in the proper administration
of justice, we must help today's jurors to obtain an intelligent picture of the evidence.

"The jurors of today themselves are better educated,
women's service has broadened their viewpoint, and
they are wise enough to understand the facts if they
are permitted to adduce them with proper help and
guidance.

"Jurors should not be made to sit silent in their boxes
like bumps on a log. I feel the need for both of these
changes is imperative."

The Judicial Council of the Bar Association, after
a full consideration of both matters, came out against
the asking of questions by jurors. It was, however,
overwhelmingly for the idea of the jurors taking notes.
I should have rested with this victory, but I was not
satisfied to leave matters in that state. I felt it necessary to press the matter to a final conclusion. I sought
to establish law upon the subject.

In view of the Supreme Court's decision, the only

way to do this was through legislative action. Hence, I have proposed a bill to be passed by our State Legislature to allow jurors to take notes. To date, nothing has come of this proposal, although it has practically the unanimous support of the bench and bar in our state.

I was gratified when the University of Michigan had its Law Review make an analysis of the situation. To our surprise, they found seven cases, going back as far as 1874, favorable to the taking of notes by jurors, so my proposal had its precedents after all.

The Michigan Law Review in its analysis came to this conclusion:

A careful instruction would vitiate the danger of any juror misconceiving his duty. It would seem that whether or not the court should voluntarily request the jury to take notes should rest in the sound discretion of the trial judge. If the court, after thorough examination of the pleadings, finds highly complex questions of fact or deeply involved issues of law to exist and believes in the exercise of its sound discretion that note taking might better enable the jury to reach a proper verdict, the court should be permitted to carefully instruct the jurors that those who believe they can better serve the court by note taking may do so.

I feel that we will be able to administer justice more ably when we rid ourselves of some of the rules of the dead past and streamline our methods and procedure. Surely, the taking of notes by jurors is high on the list.

The principal objection of note-taking is that the average laymen does not have the ability to take intelligent notes. But this argument goes back to the days when members of the juries were often illiterate. It has no validity today when we have standards for jury qualification.

It has also been argued that a juror might be absorbed in writing his notes concerning a previous statement, and then miss an important remark from the stand. It is well known that the human mind "listens" ahead of the manual writing and is capable of both functions as long as the writing is not extensive. At the worst, it is unlikely that more than one or two jurors would miss the same point. Some say that the notes can be bad notes; I would only add that memories can be worse.

Some judges in the past have gone so far as to assert that taking of notes by jurors constituted misconduct. Far from being charged with misconduct, those jurors should be praised for showing enough interest in the case to try to keep the facts straight so that justice would be done.

It has also been said that "jurors should impress the evidence on the tablets of their memories." It would be much better today if they wrote it on tablets of paper in front of them, to diminish at least the chance of their memories playing tricks on them. It has correctly been pointed out that a jury may at any time call for transcripts of any evidence it wants. I submit that a juror may not even be able to remember, at the end of a trial, just what point it was that caught his attention if he was not allowed to make a note of it at the time.

Jurors not permitted to take notes, must still rely upon their memory for the salient facts. To me it seems a mockery of justice to witness a case where there are voluminous documents, where the lawyers on both sides use up pad after pad taking notes during the course of the trial—and where only the jury must rely upon its memory. If we are willing to go to great lengths to be sure our juries arrive at impartial verdicts, then we should allow them all the facilities possible to aid in reaching the just verdict.

CHAPTER 18

ARE MARRIAGES MADE
IN HEAVEN?

~~~~~~

A REPORTER was visiting my class in Domestic Relations at the Cleveland Marshall Law School one
evening when I said, "If it were not for children in
some families, for religion in others, for economic
security with more, and—lastly and most importantly—
for fear of one's neighbors, we would have a great
many more divorces."

The next day, the newspaper headline read:

JUDGE SILBERT SAYS LOVE
AFTER MARRIAGE IS BUNK!

You would be surprised how many individuals and
organizations rose to the defense of love—and to abuse
virulently the judge who had "attacked" it. The correction the newspaper printed only spread the original
misquotation still farther.

But there was at least one bright spot—a note from a woman who wrote:

"Dear Judge, I read where you said that love after marriage is the bunk. I have been married 20 years and ain't it true!"

Newspapers love the stories that come out of Divorce Court—which really means that you, the reader, love those stories. An old one I remember concerned the divorce case of Captain Herman Archer, the real-life hero of Richard Harding Davis's "Captain Macklin." What really defeated the glamorous captain, however, was another book about his life, this one called, "Mr. Archer, U.S.A.," by R. H. Platt, Jr. Although this book never achieved the fame that Davis's did, it got an extensive reading in our courtroom, particularly the chapter where Captain Archer set down his rules for an Army wife. Alas for the captain, his wife had been a good wife, by his own standards, and I could not see fit to grant his divorce.

One colorful newspaper account of this case read:

AMERICA'S WORST HUSBAND

HE WAS SOLDIER OF FORTUNE HERO
FOR TWO FAMOUS ADVENTURE BOOKS
AND HAS FOUGHT ALL OVER THE MAPS,
BUT THE RULES HE LAID DOWN
FOR A SOLDEIR'S WIFE'S CONDUCT
WERE THE MOST PECULIAR EVER HEARD

Captain Herman N. Archer, sometimes considered America's most romantic military figure—soldier of fortune, adventurer wherever the American flag has seen earth—was called America's worst husband in a Cleveland courtroom not long ago. It happened during the dashing captain's suit for divorce from his wife, Annie Laurie Archer, a dancing teacher of San Francisco.

Common Pleas Judge Samuel H. Silbert, who heard the case, handed down an opinion as unique as the case itself.

"Uncle Sam has certainly turned out a captivating, fascinating, romantic, able soldier," commented Judge Silbert, "but I can't hand Uncle Sam a compliment for any part he may have had in the making of a husband. America's most romantic soldier is almost America's poorest husband." For this reason, the court refused to grant Captain Archer his divorce, and ordered him to pay his wife $50 a month.

Perhaps the most unusual event in this most unusual case came when the court offered Mrs. Archer freedom from this "worst husband." She refused it flatly. She still loved her romantic soldier of fortune, still wanted to be known as the wife of this hero, now military instructor at Princeton University. . . . For days the divorce court room echoed to strange tales of Captain Archer's life during the last 30 years—tales to be found in the books about him. . .

Captain Archer had, in 1923, very unwisely sat himself down to dictate a little chapter of rules for a soldier's wife.

And it was these very rules and enlarged para-

graphs on what a soldier of fortune has a right to
expect of a wife which, read in open court by
Attorney Joseph Mellen, representing the defendant, Annie Laurie Archer, caused Judge Silbert
to prick up the judicial ears and render a snappy
opinion which had the town in admiration and
mirth.

"*Not every woman can be the wife of a soldier.*"
So read Attorney Mellen from the red book. "*In
the first place, she can't get married to a furnished
flat or a few square feet of ground, she's got to
agree to marrying the map.*"

"Mrs. Archer certainly did all of that," commented the judge in his opinion. "She should
make a good map maker or command a high position with Cook's tours. I cannot agree with Captain Archer that even a soldier's wife must marry
the map. Any woman has a right to home, even
if a home constantly on the move."

Attorney Mellen continued reading—

"*A soldier's wife can't be skittish about her old
man not turning up. . . Even if he's out with some
other girl, that's all right, too. His wife's just got
to get that straight at the start—if she does, she'll
do.*"

However good the literary style of "Archer's
Wifely Rules," they evidently were not written in
a vein to convince a divorce judge, for Judge
Silbert's opinion was that—

"Even the wife of a soldier has the inalienable
right of all wives to an accounting from husbands

as to what they were doing, where they were, and whom they saw."

The evidence brought out at the trial proved, moreover, that Mrs. Archer was anything but "skittish." For ten years, she permitted Archer to introduce her as "Miss Davis" to the young lady with whom he was "keeping company." She borrowed money to keep him in uniforms, and taught dancing; she even gave lessons to other lady friends. All in all, according to Archer's own rules for marriage, Annie Laurie was a perfect wife.

Which proves that in Divorce Court as in politics, books can be enemies!

One of the most miserly men I ever encountered in a divorce case made his wife walk around the house in her bare feet to save wear on the carpets. At least he was consistently stingy. I divorced one wealthy man not once but four times. When he was sober he was stingy; when he got drunk he threw his money around like an Eastern potentate. Whenever he felt a drinking spree coming on, he telephoned a group of friends and set off on a non-stop tour of the bars. Occasionally the morning-after hangover included a wife. As soon as he sobered up he came to court for a divorce.

His last spree must have been a humdinger, because this time when he awoke he found himself on a liner en route to Europe, the inevitable new wife with him. The settlement she got should have quenched his thirst forever. At least I haven't had his divorce business since.

Some men are so stubborn about paying alimony that they will stay in jail for months before they will pay one cent to their former wives. One fellow who had hidden $19,000 rather than pay anything to his wife, sat in jail until his brother finally came to court and secretly made a settlement to get him out.

But the most stubborn case on local record—and you can find similar cases in almost any other major city in the country—was that of a doctor with a fine practice. His wife divorced him and was awarded alimony, but the doctor refused to pay. He didn't mind a bit when he was jailed for contempt of court. He treated his stay behind bars as a lark and even formed an anti-alimony club among fellow prisoners who were jailed for the same thing. This won him national publicity, even though it ruined his medical practice. That did not seem to bother him. Anything was better than paying his hated former wife a penny.

Not all husbands resent paying alimony. Once, after I said everything I could to convince a man that he was married to a fine woman—but to no avail—I agreed to give them a divorce, and I said to the woman:

"I'll therefore give you the sum of $40 per month."

The man looked at me thoughtfully for a moment.

"That's mighty fine of you judge," he said. "And to show you I'm not as bad as you think, I'll give her a couple of bucks myself."

A shocking number of women, married a short time, seem to feel that the mere fact of their marriage entitles them to alimony. As far as I am concerned, no wife is entitled to alimony unless she has enriched her husband in some way by her efforts—by bearing and raising children or by some other constructive contribution to the marriage.

It has been axiomatic from time immemorial that if you give nothing, you should get nothing. The exception to the rule seems to be in divorce court. The case of Groh - v - Groh was a classic of this kind.

I examined the facts in the Groh case closely. Here was a twenty-three-year-old woman, in good health, who had held a good position prior to her marriage—which was only of one month's duration—and who refused to be reconciled when her husband sought reconciliation. All she wanted after less than thirty days of marriage was a divorce and alimony.

Not infrequently, women who file suits for divorce and alimony make the claim that they are in poor health; the man who is sued and doesn't want to pay usually claims that he is poor and in financial distress.

The Groh marriage, however, had been of such short duration that neither could possibly present such a claim; neither had a chance to become ill or impoverished as a result of the marriage. But the wife thought she was entitled to alimony as a matter of right, merely because the parties had been married. In my decision I said:

Alimony is much misunderstood, and the subject should be made very clear by our courts. By alimony we mean allowance, a sort of pension granted by the court, and it comes by reason of the fact that either party to the marriage has enriched the other as a direct result of their marriage. One may enrich the other in the marital relation with work, with love, with effort, with affection, with loyalty and with devotion. One may do so with full and unstinted co-operation in the joint venture we call love and marriage. [It is not enough] merely to have a license, and this is true even though they are occupying the relationship of husband and wife.

Marriage cannot be founded merely on crass or sordid considerations. It must be founded on love, and upon spiritual values. Marriage implies mutual helpfulness, devotion and cooperation, a partnership for life, of the body and the spirit.

People must come to the realization that they are not entitled to alimony as a matter of course. If we were to allow alimony merely because the parties are legally married—if that is all there is to marriage—there would be nothing to make the marriage sacred; all they would have to do to start collecting would be to get a license, get married, and start out collecting and then continue collecting ad infinitum for the rest of their lives.

We must discard the theory that a marriage license is the same as a collection license. It doesn't come with the marriage fee.

That is an erroneous view of marriage. And the sooner we correct this impression, as firmly as we possibly can, the sooner perhaps our marriages will take on a more serious hue and last longer. Making a permanent meal ticket, predicated on a marriage license would be racketeering with our emotions; it would be taking and not giving, and would not be marriage, and in my opinion contrary to public policy.

I insist that if the wife has not enriched her hus-

band by love, affection, devotion and spiritual
contribution of some form, that she is not entitled
to alimony as a matter of course. The better course
for her would be to let her get a job and go to
work. It will help her to see matters more clearly;
and take marriage more seriously the next time;
if there is a next time.

That was the decision I rendered. It is still the law
in my courtroom.

He was fully eighty years old when he came before
me asking for a divorce. It was an uncontested case;
the wife was not present.

He told of a long and happy married life, of raising
children who had made good marriages. But now, "in
the sunset of life," as his lawyer termed it, his wife
refused to comfort him or be his companion or even
live with him.

He could not change her mind, he said. He was a
man of means who had always given her a good home,
and even now was giving her money and other material
things so that she could live out her years in comfort
even if she wouldn't spend them with him. Tears rolled
down his cheeks.

He stepped down from the witness stand and his
minister, who had known him for forty years, testified
as his character witness. Then a corroborating witness
offered his testimony and the case was over.

I was touched. Here was a truly pathetic case. Of
course I granted the divorce.

I couldn't get the old man out of my mind, so alone
and so sad in the final years of his life. Thus when I
saw his lawyer about a month afterward, I could not

refrain from discussing the case with him, telling him of my feelings.

The lawyer seemed so embarrassed that I asked him what the trouble was.

"Judge, I felt the same way you did when the case was heard in court," he said apologetically.

"But that was only a month ago," I reminded him. "What makes it different now?"

"Nothing," he sighed, "only the day after you signed the journal entry granting him his divorce this eighty-year-old man went right out and married an eighteen-year-old girl."

The couple were divorced in 1919 and there was a child, a baby, and after twenty-six years the case came back into court to drive home to me the thought that Dickens was right when he said, "Law, thou art an ass." Indeed, neither lawyers nor doctors nor bankers have anything to feel proud about in this case.

The court awarded custody of the fourteen-month-old daughter to the mother; the father was ordered to pay his ex-wife $3,500 a year for life, or until she re-married, in which case the "support" money would be reduced. The money was to be handled by a bank, as trustee. There was no reason to foresee that this commonplace arrangement would not work out.

Four years later, in 1923, the husband was declared incompetent by a court in Massachusetts, where he was then living. The Ohio bank was named trustee of the husband's personal estate, which amounted to more than half a million dollars, as well as of the money for the child's support.

From the time she was a baby, the daughter had

shown signs of having inherited her father's emotional weakness. She was headstrong, unmanageable and unstable.

When she was eighteen, her mother decided to send her away to school. She asked the bank, as trustee, to give her the necessary money from the support fund. The bank refused and the mother took the case to the County Probate Court—the court where matters having to do with wills and estates are settled. The court ordered the bank to pay the money, but the bank appealed the decision on the grounds that Probate Court did not have jurisdiction.

The bank's appeal was successful. The higher court declared that the case must be heard in Divorce Court. The outcome, however, was the same. The Divorce Court also ordered the bank to pay for the girl's education. Furthermore, the jurisdiction of the Divorce Court, rather than Probate Court, over the case seemed to be settled.

Unfortunately the girl's condition did not improve but rather grew worse. She had to be removed from the private school because she proved to be such a disturbing element. Next her mother tried making a home for her in a small town in New York, hoping life in the country might be beneficial. This move was no more successful. At times the girl was bright and vivacious, at other times disagreeable and vicious. She had no regard for others' personal property. She was abnormally extravagant. During these early years she attempted suicide at least three times, climbing onto window ledges or taking narcotics.

In 1939, at the age of twenty, the girl was placed in a mental hospital. After fifteen months she was released, not because she was better but because it was felt that further institutional treatment would only worsen her condition.

Again her mother decided to try taking the girl to a new environment, and they went to Bermuda. There the daughter met a twenty-three-year-old lieutenant in the British Navy. He fell in love with her and asked for her hand. The mother felt the marriage might prove beneficial to her daughter, but she dutifully told the lieutenant about her daughter's history. He still wanted to marry her, and in 1941 he did so.

For a time, the girl seemed much improved, but soon after their marriage she began to show the old signs. She took to going to bed for long periods of time; she cursed and she raged; she showed herself completely incapable of handling money. She was brought back here where, incredibly in the face of her history, doctors decided that she and the lieutenant should try having children. In 1942 the first of two children of this marriage were born. But this didn't help either, and finally in 1943, a conservator was appointed over her.

In the meantime the girl's mother and husband, trying every way they could to help her, had gone heavily into debt on her account. When it came to the point where they desperately needed financial help, they appealed to the court, asking for a modification of the twenty-six-year-old divorce decree. The case came before me in Divorce Court in 1944.

This case brought up an interesting question: May a married woman who is past the age of majority, and who is mentally incompetent, procure support from a parent who is likewise incompetent but fully capable of supporting her? (Remember that the bank was not only trustee of the girl's money but of the father's $604,000.) Also, may the husband or the mother of this incompetent woman maintain an independent claim against this defending parent (the father) for unusual and extraordinary expenditures and advances made by them in behalf of this incompetent?

I believed they could, and that I was justified in granting an allowance to take care of the increased needs of the girl. I felt that, being incompetent, she was entitled to be supported by her parents. The girl, after all, had been given an increased allowance when she was eighteen. And you will remember that at that time, in 1936, our Court of Appeals had stated that Divorce Court was the proper agency to grant this.

There was vigorous objection on the part of the estate's trustees, who appealed my ruling.

And then a strange thing happened. The Ohio Supreme Court reversed my decision. Not on the grounds that it was wrong to give her an increased award for unpaid medical bills and funds to take care of her future needs, but on the grounds that Divorce Court did not have proper jurisdiction!

Ironically, when the father died, his daughter, his only child, would inherit his entire fortune of $604,000, plus whatever the money earned. Surely if the father had been competent and without guardian he would have rallied to the support and care of his only child. A trustee, standing legally in the father's shoes, should likewise have the same feeling.

True, it is the duty of a trustee to protect the estate— and his fee pays him well for this. But is it the trustee's duty to resist an honest claim on a technicality?

A strange thing. In 1936, our higher court ordered the case into Divorce Court on the ground that only it had jurisdiction. Eight years later, when the case was again brought to Divorce Court, the decision was reversed on the grounds that it did *not* have jurisdiction!

In the meantime, while waiting for the inheritance, the mother and husband continued to scrape along on the money awarded twenty-six years ago in the original divorce decree. The girl was institutionalized and the father given custody of the two children. It is hard to imagine a worse-handled case—by the legal, the banking or the medical profession.

A June, 1951 divorce case. *Hear the Plaintiff*—

Her husband was indifferent to her, much preferring to listen to baseball commentators. He slept in the same double bed with her but did not demand or require sexual relations. For weeks and months at a time, even when she became assertive and aggressive, he still ignored her, rebuffing and humiliating her with his neglect and indifference. They had been married just three years. The husband was in his early twenties.

Hear more from the plaintiff—

He rebuffed her natural and normal requirements both by word and action, advancing captious reasons for his gross neglect of duty in this regard. In the summer he told her it was too hot. In the winter he spurned her under the pretext that her feet were too cold. Despite her embarrassment she would feel the need to take the initiative; then he would turn his back to her and move to the other end of the bed.

The husband didn't deny the charges. According to

the wife, he apparently felt that she was too affectionate and demonstrative altogether, unduly stressing sex
in marriage.

The wife brought her suit for divorce on grounds of
extreme cruelty and gross neglect and she bluntly
spelled out extreme cruelty and gross neglect as sexual
maladjustment.

Now that's the basis for many of our divorce cases,
but seldom is it detailed so explicitly. More often it is
hidden under some other grounds for divorce. But this
woman was without pretense or false shame. She
alleged that as a result of such gross misconduct she
had become nervous, restless, frustrated and ill. She
contended that her husband was cruel, therefore,
causing her mental anguish and extreme unhappiness.
Her only remedy was divorce, she said.

So the question before me was: How far may a man
go in ignoring his wife and her marital requirements
(or vice versa)? Assuming he had abstained from sex
for long periods of time, would that constitute gross
neglect?

Technically, gross neglect of duty might be defined
legally as any neglect or omission on the part of either
spouse toward the other in the marital relationship.
It is a broad term, loosely used even by lawyers. In
general, it is held to include any breach of consequence
in the marital relationship. The duty referred to must
not be of a trifling character but must be a duty that
is germaine and of a quality which amounts to gross
neglect. It may consist of various acts or omissions
over a stated period.

Is sexual intercourse an essential in marriage? Or
will mere courtesy, consideration and financial support

fill the bill enough to satisfy the law's requirements? Assuming the parties are young and potent, will the continued indifference and failure to cohabit constitute a neglect of duty that is gross?

For a married man to say that because he supports his wife he has done his duty toward her is to state what is not the fact. The saying, "We do not live by bread alone," is particularly significant of marriage. The wife is entitled to her husband's devotion and affection; it is part of the conjugal bliss in marriage.

To declare that one does his full duty by furnishing common necessities and common courtesies toward the other is to misunderstand completely the true meaning of marriage. Parents and relatives can do that as well as husbands or wives. Marriage implies the physical and the spiritual contacts between those of the opposite sex.

We have entertained a fetish about discussing sex openly. Even our courts have glossed over the subject although we know full well that the Church sanctifies marriage and that the State regulates, controls and protects it. Marriage is not a sordid sex arrangement but a holy spiritual union. It is beautiful and necessary to keep the parties loyal and bound to each other, and for the proper propagation and natural evolution of the human race. You cannot have a happy marriage without sexual satisfaction. If more men and women learned that, there would be fewer divorces.

For a husband wilfully to refuse to gratify his wife's sexual desires and requirements would be against public policy. It would be cruelty and gross neglect toward her. Were there a constant and insistent demand for sex, it would be one matter, but for a man (or a woman) to remain passive and indifferent and to refuse to participate in sexual relations at normal instances indefinitely would make for a conduct, or lack of conduct, as would constitute gross neglect. If the husband were persistent about such conduct it could be extreme cruelty as well as gross neglect.

If the parties had become old or incapable of having sexual relations it would be one thing. Where they were young and vigorous and did nothing more gratifying than turn their backs on sexual intercourse, that would be wholly different and would constitute neglect of duty and extreme cruelty.

Even frigidity and mild forms of impotency can be cured today. The least the defendant could have done was to seek medical aid had he required it. His contention was that he didn't require it, that he was merely indifferent to sexual intercourse.

It has been held generally that excessive sexual demands constitute extreme cruelty. There was no reason in this case for holding that wilful refusal to gratify normal sexual demands and needs was less than extreme cruelty.

Today with doctors, psychiatrists and scientists available, sexual frigidity and indifference can and should be treated and cured. For young married people to ignore the problem is to make a tragedy of their marriage and constitutes the grossest kind of neglect.

Therefore I ruled for the first time that sexual intercourse is an essential in marriage—and that abstinence was gross neglect of duty—gross enough to entitle the party to a divorce, in my courtroom anyway.

Louis Seltzer and I have been friends ever since he was

a cherub-faced cub reporter and I a member of the police prosecutor's staff. Our friendship has managed to survive these fifty years, but it hasn't always been easy. On one occasion, Mrs. Silbert and I attended a wedding reception; the bride had a bootlegging record, which probably should have deterred us, but it didn't. During the afternoon, however, a fight developed, and we quickly left.

The next day Louis Seltzer's *Cleveland Press* reported that Mrs. Silbert was one of those bopped over the head with a whiskey bottle during that colorful social event.

This was nothing, though, compared to the time Louis' paper made me the unwitting butt of one of its crusades—while I sentenced him for contempt of court.

And the real irony of it all was that I was the one who had suggested the story in the first place.

Although Cleveland has the reputation of being a family kind of a city in a family kind of a state (no one ever called us a middle western Reno), our divorce procedures (as well as our divorce laws) leave a lot to be desired. One of the things that bothered some of the other judges and myself was the assembly-line or "divorce mill" aspect of the process. Very often I have had to handle as many as fifty divorces a day, along with my other duties. On one occasion that none of us will forget, nine judges handled 215 divorce cases in two hours!

I had often urged Louis to throw his paper's weight into a crusade to change this system. Little did I know that when he did, I would emerge as the "villain," although the paper carefully pointed out that the fault lay with the system and not with the judge. But I am

getting ahead of the story. All I knew when I picked
up my *Cleveland Press* on January 31, 1949, was that
the headline that struck me between the eyes said:

"It is possible to obtain a divorce in Cuyahoga
County:

"Without either of the marriage partners appearing
before a judge. . .

"Without witnesses. . .

"Without presentation of a shred of evidence that a
divorce is justified. . .

"Without a six-week's cooling off period. . ."

Louis and his city editor, Louis Clifford, had decided that an exposé of the divorce process would be
the best (or at least the most dramatic) way of bringing the problem to the attention of the voters. Leonard
Hammer, a reporter one who was well known around
the courthouse, was assigned to the story.

Hammer started out by inventing a name for himself—C. P. Ress. (C for Cleveland, P. Ress for Press.)
As Mr. Ress, a lawyer, Hammond filed a divorce
petition. He had it signed by Mrs. Richard R. Camp-
bell, the happily married young wife of the *Press'*
make-up editor. (They joined in the "test" in case real
persons were needed at any time.) When Hammer
had attended to these preliminaries, he prepared a
decree and inserted it among those papers on my desk
that had reached the stage where they were simply
awaiting my signature to make the divorces final.

And I signed the phony divorce.

It was fraud, pure and simple. Furthermore, as one
columnist wrote, the only thing it proved was that
Hammer, a reporter, had a great deal of freedom to
wander around the judges' chambers.

My initial reaction was, not unexpectedly, anger—in spite of the *Press*'s statement that I "just happened" to be the victim. "This should not stand as a reflection on Judge Silbert's record of long service as a jurist . . . the same thing would have happened no matter what judge was sitting in divorce court. The fault is with the court, not the judge."

Nevertheless, I might have been tempted to let the whole affair alone had not both my colleagues and the lawyers who practiced before our courts felt that to ignore the "exposé" would be damaging to the dignity of the court. So the story ended with my finding the parties involved guilty of contempt of court, and fining them $1,000. Before doing so, Louis and I each made statements attributing only the highest of misguided motives to each other.

As for the Campbells, they found themselves divorced, and so had to get married all over again. To make doubly sure that they weren't penalized, I vacated their phony (but real!) divorce at the time of the contempt hearings. And as for me, I've never been able to hold a grudge. When Hammer was later fired by the *Press*, I was delighted to write a job reference for him.

No one can set down ten rules for a happy marriage and say, "If you meet these standards, your marriage will last. If you don't, you'll end up in Divorce Court." But on the whole, from my experience with thousands and thousands of divorce cases, I think I can safely state a few general rules for *starting* a marriage. If a marriage is built on a solid foundation, it will survive

many of the vicissitudes that send husbands and wives
into court.

I do not believe in early marriage, although I would
never set an arbitrary, exact age at which it is proper
to marry. If the man has a job and a little money in
the bank, he may be ready to get married. If the couple
must go into debt to marry—even if the debt is to their
parents—the chances are they are too young. The debts
that come from installment buying and babies they
can't afford strangle young marriages.

"Love at first sight" is just as likely to be grounds for
divorce as it is for marriage. If you think you have
fallen in love, wait. Find out whether it is a passing
romance or a real love before you get married, not
after. The couple truly in love has nothing to lose by
waiting. The couple only infatuated has everything to
lose by not waiting. Don't marry on impulse.

No matter what the grounds for divorce are called,
they all boil down to some form of incompatability.
A man and woman are less likely to be incompatable
if they have at least some things in common—a simi-
larity of background, education, religion and interests.
It is a rare marriage that can survive no common de-
nominator.

And yet a man and woman can pass all of these
tests and still be candidates for divorce. Which brings
us right back to the divorce courts. Here is where they
call me an authority. Since I have taught divorce law
for thirty years and have granted 80,000 divorces, and
have settled tens of thousands amicably, I accept the
designation.

Legally and socially, I think we handle divorce
miserably.

Our divorce laws in the United States are an unbelievable hodgepodge. What one state calls "grounds"
another laughs out of court. Can you imagine what
chaos there would be in the business world if every
state had its own laws to cover contracts, negotiable
instruments and other commitments?

Yet we apparently don't rate marriage or divorce as
importantly as we do business, although there is a lot
of talk about how sacred it is. Indeed, the fact that one
can "shop around" among the states for a law to suit
one's needs or pocketbook is not only admitted—it is
encouraged.

I once had a man before me who, although anxious
to get rid of his wife, couldn't meet even our easy Ohio
standards. When I told him that I could not in good
conscience grant him a divorce, he simply took a train
for Reno. With the feeling that I should not permit this
farce, I wrote to a Reno judge, telling him the true
facts of the case.

"You may be right," the judge wrote back, "but we
need the business here."

In Ohio we have ten grounds for divorce, the most
common of which are "extreme cruelty" and "gross
neglect of duty." Extreme cruelty covers "mental
anguish," and mental anguish seems to cover just about
anything, as long as you can bring along two witnesses
to prove it. Other grounds include wilful absence for
a period of three years and habitual drinking for three
years. I have never been able to understand the value
our legislature places on the continuous-time element.
Why is a three-year drunk so much worse than a two-
year-ten-month drunk?

Of course, we also grant divorces on the grounds of

adultery, but since we demand proof, adultery isn't used very often. As the old joke has it, it isn't the adultery they mind, it's the bother of finding the witnesses.

All of this indicates that we play a legal game as far as the grounds for divorce are concerned—and we are all a party to the farce of phonying up excuses.

I would like to see uniform divorce laws based on the honest, simple presumption of incompatability. Because when you get right down to it, whether you call it adultery, mental anguish, extreme cruelty, desertion, or whatever, the only real reason for two people to get divorced is because they are incompatable.

Once we can make the legal aspect of divorce honest, I recommend that we start treating it as the social problem that it really is. And here is where I would suggest the important reforms.

Basically, our problem is not easy divorce; it is easy marriage. Therefore I would make marriage a more difficult state to enter, as is befitting its importance. I would make the hasty marriage (entered into with the knowledge that if it doesn't work out, it can be solved by the hasty divorce) harder to contract. As I said, I think this is a social problem, not just a legal one, but presumably a waiting period would have some salutatory effect on quickie marriages. I also think that if the out of an easy divorce is taken away, there might be fewer thoughtless marriages. Thus I would institute a waiting period before a divorce could be granted. I would further require that the parties to a divorce wait a year before they are permitted to remarry.

And I would pay a lawyer more for affecting a reconciliation than for obtaining a divorce.

If all attempts at conciliation fail, and if at the end of the cooling-off period both parties still want a divorce, *then* I would make it easy for them to get it—without sham or pretense or collusion—simply by pleading the truth, which is incompatability.

The worst of the collusion is that we judges are a part of it, as we sit in court soberly listening to mental anguish after mental anguish, and even more hypocritically judging the "evidence" upon which we must make our decisions. How "gross" is the cruelty of a husband who opens windows when his wife wants them closed? How much "mental anguish" is involved in whether the coffee is served with or without cream? Yet these were two actual cases. Obviously, these are not the real reasons why the couples sued for divorce. Or, if they were, then the chances are that conciliation or a cooling-off period would have held the marriages together.

Our Ohio law requires a six-weeks' delay between the filing of a divorce petition and the hearing of the case. Some years ago, I tried, informally, to extend that period to six months by juggling the docket. Some of my fellow judges followed suit, until the lawyers began raising cain with us on the grounds that we were "legislating." Technically, they were right, but look what happened while we were doing it: According to a later check-up, the divorce rate in our courts during that period dropped twenty per cent. More than 400 marriages were actually saved by that cooling-off process!

Maybe not all of them should have been saved; maybe not all of them lasted very much longer—but obviously a great many people had second thoughts

about wanting a divorce, simply because they had to
wait for one.

Among the letters I got from "made-up" marriage
partners was this one:

Dear Judge,
   If it hadn't been for your holding up the divorce, I would have been divorced and very unhappy today. I was very angry at the time when
my lawyer explained that you were holding it up,
but now I bless you. After my husband and I
quarreled we were both too proud to make up.
If it had been called in six weeks, I would still
have been mad enough to go through with it. But
about four months after my attorney filed, I
changed my mind and was worried to death for
fear the case would be called. But then one afternoon my husband called me up to wish me a
happy birthday. We went out to dinner. We made
up. We have just returned from our second honeymoon. Thanks again.

In spite of my 5,000 divorce cases a year, I guess
I am still above all a sentimentalist. But what that
letter and that whole incident really shows is that I
still believe as I did forty years ago when I wrote:

"To me, the law does not merely mean the reading
of the rules decreed by society, rattling its dry bones.
The law should possess a soul and a heart. It should
have sympathy and humanity as its basis. What counts
the most is using the law with a view of accomplish-
ing substantial justice."

Where I have erred, I hope it will always be found
that I erred on the side of my fellow man.